W9-CFB-177

The American Revolution

The American Revolution

DON NARDO

Greenhaven Press, Inc., San Diego, California

Library of Congress Cataloging-in-Publication Data

Nardo, Don, 1947–
      The American Revolution / Don Nardo.
          p.   cm. — (Opposing viewpoints digests)
      Includes bibliographical references and index.
      Summary: Offers opposing viewpoints regarding the American
      Revolution, including prewar disputes, patriot versus loyalist views,
      wartime concerns, and debate among modern historians.
          ISBN 1-56510-755-1 (lib. bdg. : alk. paper). — ISBN 1-56510-754-3
      (pbk. : alk. paper)
          1. United States—History—Revolution, 1775–1783—Juvenile
      literature. [1. United States—History—Revolution, 1775–1783.]
      I. Title. II. Series.
      E208.N25   1998
      973.3—dc21   97-49627
                                                                          CIP
                                                                           AC

Cover Photo: Peter Newark's American Pictures
The American Revolution: A Picture Sourcebook,
Dover Publications: 14, 32, 102
Library of Congress: 12, 15, 19, 21, 25,
38, 47, 53, 61, 70, 77, 79, 83, 88, 94

©1998 by Greenhaven Press, Inc.
PO Box 289009, San Diego, CA 92198-9009

Printed in the U.S.A.

CONTENTS

FOREWORD

The only way in which a human being can make some approach to knowing the whole of a subject is by hearing what can be said about it by persons of every variety of opinion and studying all modes in which it can be looked at by every character of mind. No wise man ever acquired his wisdom in any mode but this.

—John Stuart Mill

Greenhaven Press's Opposing Viewpoints Digests in history are designed to aid in examining important historical issues in a way that develops critical thinking and evaluating skills. Each book presents thought-provoking argument and stimulating debate on a single topic. In analyzing issues through opposing views, students gain a social and historical context that cannot be discovered in textbooks. Excerpts from primary sources reveal the personal, political, and economic side of historical topics such as the American Revolution, the Great Depression, and the Bill of Rights. Students begin to understand that history is not a dry recounting of facts, but a record founded on ideas—ideas that become manifest through lively discussion and debate. Digests immerse students in contemporary discussions: Why did many colonists oppose a bill of rights? What was the original intent of the New Deal and on what grounds was it criticized? These arguments provide a foundation for students to assess today's debates on censorship, welfare, and other issues. For example, *The Great Depression: Opposing Viewpoints Digests* offers opposing arguments on controversial issues of the time as well as views and interpretations that interest modern historians. A major debate during Franklin D. Roosevelt's administration was whether the president's New Deal programs would lead to a permanent welfare state, creating a citizenry dependent on government money. *The Great Depression* covers this issue from both historical and modern perspectives, allowing students to critically evaluate arguments both in the context of their time and through the benefit of historical hindsight.

This emphasis on debate makes Digests a useful tool for writing reports, research papers, and persuasive essays. In addition to supplying students with a range of possible topics and supporting material, the Opposing Viewpoints Digests offer unique features through which young readers acquire and sharpen critical thinking and reading skills. To assure an appropriate and consistent reading level for young adults, all essays in each volume are written by a single author. Each essay heavily quotes readable primary sources that are fully cited to allow for further research and documentation. Thus, primary sources are introduced in a context to enhance comprehension.

In addition, each volume includes extensive research tools, including a section comprising excerpts from original documents pertaining to the issue under discussion. In *The Bill of Rights*, for example, readers can examine the English Magna Carta, the Virginia State Bill of Rights drawn up in 1776, and various opinions by U.S. Supreme Court justices in key civil rights cases, as well as an unabridged version of the U.S. Bill of Rights. These documents both complement the text and give students access to a wide variety of relevant sources in a single volume. Additionally, a "facts about" section allows students to peruse facts and statistics that pertain to the topic. These statistics are also fully cited, allowing students to question and analyze the credibility of the source. Two bibliographies, one for young adults and one listing the author's sources, are also included; both are annotated to guide student research. Finally, a comprehensive index allows students to scan and locate content efficiently.

Greenhaven's Opposing Viewpoints Digests, like Greenhaven's higher level and critically acclaimed Opposing Viewpoints Series, have been developed around the concept that an awareness and appreciation for the complexity of seemingly simple issues is particularly important in a democratic society. In a democracy, the common good is often, and very appropriately, decided by open debate of widely varying views. As one of democracy's greatest advocates, Thomas Jefferson, observed, "Difference of opinion leads to inquiry, and inquiry to truth." It is to this principle that Opposing Viewpoints Digests are dedicated.

Conflicting Convictions in Prerevolutionary America

In March 1782, the British Parliament voted to abandon the war effort against Britain's thirteen American colonies, unofficially ending the American Revolutionary War, which had begun in 1775. Soon afterward, the British government opened peace negotiations in Paris with a delegation of American peace commissioners, including Benjamin Franklin (joined later by John Jay and John Adams). The representatives of the warring parties signed the preliminary treaty on November 30, 1782, and the final version on September 3, 1783. Having won independence by defeating the most powerful empire in the world, Americans could take pride in their victory and look forward to the potential blessings of peace and self-rule; and cities and towns from Maine to Georgia staged enthusiastic celebrations.

Yet not all Americans took part in these celebrations, for not all were happy about the war's outcome. Though they now resided in a new country, the United States of America, these so-called loyalists professed allegiance to the British king and considered themselves British subjects. The subsequent passage of time and great success of the United States has tended to obscure the fact that at no time during the Revolutionary War did the Americans present a completely united front against Britain. Revolutionary leader and future president John Adams estimated that shortly after the outbreak of the war only about a third of the colonists were "patriots" who endorsed opposing British policies or fighting Britain; another third were loyalists who saw the patriots as ingrates, troublemakers, or even traitors to the mother country; and the rest were indifferent, caring little who governed them. Although during the course of the war more and more

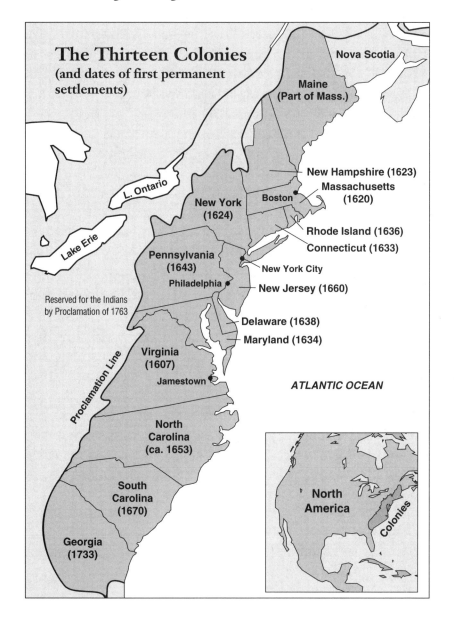

Americans became committed patriots, deep divisions remained. Nearly fifty thousand loyalists fought on the British side between 1775 and 1781. And at war's end, some eighty thousand loyalists, 2.5 percent of the American population, fled the United States rather than live in a country they considered illegitimate.[1]

Similar strong differences of opinion existed in the colonies in the crucial decade preceding the war. In this formative stage of the revolution, beginning in earnest with the Stamp Act in 1765 and ending with the outbreak of hostilities in 1775, the colonists rarely agreed on important political issues. Some argued that the British Parliament had no right to tax the colonies, for instance, while others felt that Parliament should be able to do so under certain conditions.

Furthermore, such disagreements did not develop simply along the lines of patriots versus loyalists. The patriots themselves were divided into moderate and radical camps. The moderates were represented by well-to-do aristocrats, including Thomas Jefferson and George Washington, who, even after the war's opening salvos of musket fire, hoped for some kind of reconciliation with Britain. As late as 1776, these men did not in their hearts want independence from the mother country. Rather, they desired only to be accorded their full rights as Englishmen, rights they felt that Parliament had lately unjustly abridged. By contrast, in the face of what they saw as outrageous British abuses, radicals such as Samuel Adams, Patrick Henry, and Thomas Paine argued for a split from Britain. Paine, for example, asserted that Britain taxed its American colonies in order to finance its wars; and, since Britain's wars were not America's wars, Britain and America ought to part company.

A Separate Nation at First Unthinkable

The dramatic series of events that caused the various and wide-ranging differences of opinion among the colonists began in the early 1760s, when all Americans still considered themselves loyal British subjects. Indeed, in 1763, at the conclusion of the French and Indian War against France, and only thirteen years before the signing of the American Declaration of Independence, the idea of the colonies' breaking free of the mother country was unheard-of, even unthinkable. As noted historian Samuel Eliot Morison explains, there was very little

> American nationalism or separatist feeling in the colonies prior to 1775. Americans did not start off in 1763 . . . with the conviction that they were entitled to be a separate and independent nation. They never felt . . . that they were so downtrodden by tyrannical masters as to make independence the only solution. On the contrary, Americans were not only content but proud to be part of the British imperium [empire]. But they did feel very strongly that they were entitled to all constitutional rights that Englishmen possessed in England.[2]

Thus, as long as the British government accorded Americans these rights and treated the colonies in a fair and reasonable manner, the colonists appeared content with British rule.

This situation changed rather abruptly when the colonists began to feel that the British king and Parliament were *not* treating them fairly and reasonably. In its victory over France in 1763, Britain gained huge territories in North America, among them southern Canada and the lands lying between the original thirteen colonies and the Mississippi River. To maintain control over their vast American possessions, especially in the event that France renewed hostilities, the British decided it was necessary to keep their army near its wartime strength of eighty-five regiments. The problem was that paying for these troops was a very expensive proposition.

As a partial solution to this problem, the British leadership chose to station large numbers of soldiers in America and to raise the money for their upkeep locally by taxing the colonists. The first such tax was the American Revenue Act of 1764, an altered version of an older customs duty. Foreign

In 1764 King George III and the British Parliament began taxing American colonists on imported goods such as tea, sugar, and silk.

sugar and luxury products such as wine, silk, and linen now carried stiff taxes when imported into the American colonies. Several local colonial legislatures objected to the Revenue Act; that of New York sent a petition to King George III and Parliament claiming it should be exempt from any tax not imposed by its own representatives. "Leave it to the legislative power of the colony," the petition read, "to impose all other [financial] burdens upon its own people, which the public exigencies [needs] may require."[3] North Carolina was even more blunt in a similar complaint made to its governor, objecting strongly to the "new taxes and impositions laid on us without our privy and consent, and against what we esteem our inherent right, and exclusive privilege of imposing our own taxes."[4]

"No Taxation Without Representation"

These complaints were mild, however, in comparison with the furor that arose over Parliament's 1765 Stamp Act, the first direct, internal tax Britain had ever imposed on its American colonies. "The Stamp Act," writes historian Harry M. Ward,

> placed duties on paper, vellum, and parchment to be used for public purposes. . . . All legal and business documents, certificates for clearance of ships, court proceedings, pamphlets, newspapers, playing cards, and dice had to be stamped. The stamps were in the form of impressions in relief (like a modern notary seal). The annual burden per colonist would be only about one shilling, equal to one-third of a day's labor. The program would be administered by an American Stamp Office in London; in the colonies there would be one stamp distributor for each of nine districts.[5]

American reaction to the Stamp Act was loud and often violent, as colonists from all walks of life rose in protest. In many cities angry crowds ridiculed and sometimes physically attacked fellow citizens chosen to distribute the stamps. In New York, such a crowd broke into the governor's coach house and forced the officer in charge of the stamped paper to burn it, then marched to the house of another officer, who had promised "to cram the Stamp Act down the people's throats," and ransacked the place. In Boston, irate citizens hanged the local stamp distributor in effigy and destroyed his shop. Afterward, they attacked the homes of royal tax collectors, burning furniture and tossing books and personal effects into the streets. Similar unofficial protests, staged by groups of colonists calling themselves the Sons of Liberty (or Liberty Boys), occurred throughout the American colonies.

Meanwhile, the colonial legislatures unleashed official protests. The most celebrated was that of Virginia's assembly, the House of Burgesses, spearheaded by the fiercely patriotic Patrick Henry. In an impassioned speech, Henry daringly began naming despotic rulers who had been violently removed from power. "Caesar had his Brutus," he thundered, "and Charles the First his Cromwell!" When he continued the analogy with "and George the Third—" the speaker of the house and several others tried to shout him down with cries of "Treason!" But he persevered, finishing the phrase with the words, "may profit from their example!" Henry then concluded, "If this be treason, make the most of it."[6] The House of Burgesses went on to formulate a number of resolutions, including this statement:

> The General Assembly of this colony has the only and sole exclusive right and power to lay taxes and impositions upon the inhabitants of this colony, and . . . every attempt to vest such power in any persons whatsoever other than the General assembly aforesaid has a manifest tendency to destroy British as well as American freedom.[7]

The Virginia legislature also resolved that Virginians were not bound to pay any taxes imposed from outside the colony and

The Stamp Act of 1765, which required British stamps such as these to appear on many purchased items, enraged American colonists and ignited the first spark of colonial unity.

Patrick Henry delivers a fiery speech before Virginia's assembly. Henry spear-headed the protest against taxation without representation.

that anyone advocating such taxes would be considered an enemy of Virginia. These fiery resolves were published in newspapers all over the colonies; and they helped to inspire representatives from nine of the colonies to meet in the so-called Stamp Act Congress, the first spontaneous expression of colonial unity; in October 1765, this body strongly urged Parliament to repeal the Stamp Act.

Some British leaders agreed with Henry and other angry Americans that the Stamp Act was unjust because the colonists had no representatives in Parliament, the body that had imposed the tax. As cries of "No taxation without representation" rose in America, in January 1766 William Pitt, earl of Chatham, stood before his colleagues in Parliament and urged that the act be repealed:

> The Commons of America, represented by their several assemblies, have ever been in the possession of the

exercise of this, their constitutional right, of giving and granting their own money. They would have been slaves if they had not enjoyed it. At the same time, this kingdom . . . has always bound the colonies by her laws, by her regulations, and restrictions in trade, in navigation, in manufactures, in everything, except that of taking their money out of their pockets without their consent.[8]

The Townshend Acts

Pitt and his supporters eventually prevailed and Parliament repealed the Stamp Act in March 1766. But it did so because a majority of its members felt the act could not be effectively enforced without resorting to major military force, not because of concerns that the colonists had no representation in the British legislature. Whatever motivated the repeal, the Americans were ecstatic. Celebrations erupted across the land, many of which expressed renewed feelings of loyalty to Britain. New York's assembly voted to erect a statue of George III and many grateful cities and towns set up busts of William Pitt. To the colonists, the repeal seemed to confirm that the mother country was willing to treat them, her loyal subjects, fairly and reasonably after all.

But this optimistic mood soon began to sour. The reality was that Britain still badly needed funds to support its colonial regiments. Responding to this need, in 1767 Charles Townshend, chancellor of the British exchequer (roughly equivalent to today's U.S. secretary of the treasury), proposed new duties on goods imported into the colonies from Britain, including glass, lead, paints, paper, and tea. American reaction to these Townshend Acts was reflected in the attitudes expressed in the twelve *Farmer's Letters* published in colonial newspapers late in 1767 by Philadelphia lawyer John Dickinson. After warning his readers that the Townshend duties were just as outrageous a revenue scheme as the Stamp Act, Dickinson wrote in the twelfth letter:

Let these truths be indelibly impressed on our minds—
that we cannot be happy without being free—that we
cannot be free without being secure in our property—
that we cannot be secure in our property if without our
consent others may . . . take it away—that taxes imposed on us by Parliament do thus take it away—that
duties raised for the sole purpose of raising money are
taxes—that attempts to lay such duties should be instantly and firmly opposed—that this opposition can
never be effectual unless it is the united effort of these
provinces.[9]

By calling for the colonies to present a united front against
Britain in matters of unfair taxation, Dickinson had resurrect-
ed the defiant spirit of the Stamp Act Congress and contributed to a steadily intensifying movement toward federal
union that would culminate in the birth of the United States
in 1776.

The colonies did mount a united effort to fight the Townshend duties. Their response took the form of voluntary agreements by merchants to boycott the British goods covered
under the acts and the promotion of home industries, wearing
American-made clothes, and drinking tea grown in the
colonies. The effort eventually worked, for American imports
fell by nearly a third, leading Parliament to repeal the
Townshend Acts in 1770. The one exception was the tax on
imported tea, which the British retained; but as the other taxes
had been eliminated and the colonies were otherwise enjoying
great economic prosperity, few colonists quibbled.

Although the colonies had managed to rid themselves of the
majority of the Townshend taxes, the crisis had clearly demon-
strated that colonial unity against the British was less solid
than the patriotic protesters would have liked. A number of
merchants who at first refused to sign nonimportation agreements did so reluctantly after groups of Liberty Boys threatened them or roughed them up; such intimidation tactics

alarmed many conservative colonists, pushing them further into the loyalist camp. Other merchants and ports backed out of their agreements when loyalist newspapers published articles accusing supposedly patriotic merchants of secretly smuggling British goods into the colonies. Thus were drawn the political and emotional lines that would continue to separate patriots and loyalists for more than two decades.

An Attack on One Is an Attack on All

As in the case of the Stamp Act's repeal, the elimination of the Townshend Acts seemed to return the American colonies to a state of relative normalcy. But the resistance movement sprang to life when a new crisis, by far the worst yet, gripped America early in 1774. The trouble originated with the retained tax on imported tea, a product many Americans had continued to boycott. In May 1773, Parliament passed an act allowing the British East India Company to bypass Britain and sell its tea directly to the American colonies at a reduced price (since the usual duty charged by British ports was now eliminated). This imposed no new tax on imported tea in America; however, wary colonial radicals interpreted the move as an attempt to bribe American boycotters into buying the tea and paying the duty. Accordingly, resistance mounted; in three of the four major ports that received tea shipments— New York, Philadelphia, and Charleston—locals halted importation of the tea or sent it back.

The scenario in the fourth port—Boston—was quite different. Local patriots demanded that the colonial governor, Thomas Hutchinson, send the tea ships back. When he refused, on December 16, 1773, a band of Liberty Boys dressed up as Mohawk Indians marched to the waterfront and dumped 342 chests of tea into the harbor. There was no violence and no one was injured; on December 23 the *Massachusetts Gazette* reported that after the incident, by now referred to as the Boston Tea Party, the city of Boston "was very quiet during the whole evening and night following."[10]

This quiet proved to be the lull before the storm, however. King George and most of his subjects in England were outraged at what they saw as a willful and unforgivable destruction of property. Prodded by this outrage, Parliament proceeded to play directly into the hands of the American radicals, who were hoping that the Tea Party would instigate a confrontation with the British. The retaliation took the form of the Coercive (or Intolerable) Acts, passed between March and June 1774. Among these were the Boston Port Act, which closed the port of Boston until such time as the colonists paid for the lost tea; the Massachusetts Government and Administration of Justice Act, which placed harsh restrictions on the powers of local government; and the Quartering Act, which allowed the royal governor to quarter British troops in colonial homes.

Parliament had hoped that the Coercive Acts would isolate and make an example of Massachusetts, thereby discouraging any further colonial resistance to British policies. But the acts had the opposite effect, galvanizing the colonies in a united stance against what large numbers of Americans saw as clear-cut abuses. News of Boston's plight spread via the communication

American colonists dressed as Mohawk Indians staged the Boston Tea Party to declare the tax on tea intolerable.

network of the "committees of correspondence," groups organized earlier to keep all colonies informed about various American-British crises. In defiance of the blockade, other colonies sent thousands of bushels of corn and wheat and tons of other relief supplies to beleaguered Boston. Meanwhile, on May 17, eighty-nine members of Virginia's House of Burgesses, among them George Washington, Thomas Jefferson, and Patrick Henry, met in the Raleigh Tavern in Williamsburg and declared:

> We are . . . clearly of [the] opinion, that an attack made on one of our sister colonies, to compel submission to arbitrary taxes, is an attack made on all British America, and threatens ruin to the rights of all, unless the united wisdom of the whole be applied. And for this purpose it is recommended to the committee of correspondence, that they communicate, with their several corresponding committees, on the expediency of appointing deputies from the several colonies . . . to meet in general Congress.[11]

The First Continental Congress

Responding to this call for unity, the members of the committees organized what became known as the First Continental Congress. Meeting in Philadelphia in September 1774, fifty-six delegates from twelve of the thirteen colonies tried to formulate a response to what they viewed as growing threats to American liberty. Clearly, all saw the Boston Tea Party and institution of the retaliatory Coercive Acts as a crucial turning point in relations between the colonies and the mother country. As Samuel Morison puts it, the main question was now one of power:

> Who would rule, or have the final say? All other questions of taxation, customs duties, and the like faded into the background. Through all stages [of the revolutionary events that followed], the dominant issue was

The First Continental Congress convenes in Philadelphia to discuss the building tension between the colonies and Britain.

one of power—should Britain or America dictate the terms of their mutual association, or separation? Could these opposing claims of authority and freedom ever be reconciled?[12]

Most of the members of the Continental Congress did not consider themselves extremists or agitators and did not seriously contemplate the idea of separating from Britain, an attitude shared by most colonists. Some of the delegates, Samuel Adams and Patrick Henry perhaps most prominent among them, were clearly radicals who thought a complete split with the mother country was inevitable. But the majority, referred to at the time as reconciliationists (because they hoped to reconcile with Britain), only wanted Parliament and the king to repeal the Coercive Acts, stop trying to tax the colonies, and in general act more reasonably. Moderate patriots like Virginia's

Thomas Jefferson and John Jay of New York desired a fair settlement with Britain and continued to reaffirm their allegiance to the mother country.

One avenue of reconciliation the congress considered was revising the relationship between Britain and the colonies. On September 28, Joseph Galloway of Pennsylvania introduced his Plan of Union, which proposed to settle the power problem by creating an American version of Parliament. That body and the British Parliament would have veto powers over each other in matters pertaining to the American colonies. The new colonial government, Galloway suggested, would "be administered by a President-General to be appointed by the King, and a Grand Council to be chosen by the representatives of the people of the several colonies in their respective assemblies, once in every three years." [13]

The delegates ultimately tabled Galloway's plan for reconciliation, however, for the mood of the meeting had already taken a more radical turn. In mid-September, Massachusetts patriot Paul Revere had arrived with the stunning news of the Suffolk Resolves, drafted by Joseph Warren and passed on September 9 by a clandestine meeting of towns in the Boston area. These statements, the most brazen yet made by Americans against the British, called the Coercive Acts "gross infractions of those rights to which we are justly entitled by the laws of nature" and declared that "no obedience is due from this province [colony] to either or any part of the acts," which were "attempts of a wicked administration to enslave America." [14] The Suffolk Resolves also urged Massachusetts to form its own government in defiance of the royal governor, recommended a near total economic boycott of British goods, and called for the people to arm themselves in preparation for possible fighting.

The Continental Congress endorsed the Suffolk Resolves. Even Galloway and the other conservatives went along for fear that opposition would be interpreted as taking the British side. Later, on October 14, the congress issued its own re-

solves, stating bluntly that the American colonies were "entitled to life, liberty, and property, and that they have never
ceded to any sovereign power whatever a right to dispose of
either without their consent." The congress also listed all of
the acts passed by the British since 1763 that it deemed offen-
sive and illegal and demanded their repeal. Nevertheless, the
document in no way threatened separation from Britain and
even held out hope for eventual reconciliation, concluding
that the delegates hoped "that their fellow-subjects in Great
Britain will . . . restore us to that state in which both countries
found happiness and prosperity."[15]

The Fateful Struggle Begins

At least one influential man in Britain considered the resolves
and demands coming from Philadelphia both decent and just.
On January 20, 1775, distressed at the continued deterioration
of relations between his country and its American colonies,
William Pitt pleaded the American cause to Parliament's
House of Lords. "I contend not for indulgence, but justice to
America," he urged:

> Let the sacredness of their property remain inviolate;
> let it be taxable only by their own consent, given in their
> provincial assemblies, else *it will cease to be property*. . . .
> [American] resistance to your acts was necessary as it
> was just; and your vain declarations of the omnipo-
> tence of Parliament, and your imperious doctrines of
> the necessity of submission, will be found equally impo-
> tent to convince, or to enslave your fellow-subjects in
> America. . . . Look at the papers transmitted [to] us
> from America; when you consider their decency, firm-
> ness, and wisdom, you cannot but respect their cause,
> and wish to make it your own. . . . For solidity of rea-
> soning . . . and wisdom of conclusion . . . no nation, or
> body of men, can stand in preference to the general
> Congress at Philadelphia. I trust it is obvious to your
> Lordships that all attempts to impose servitude upon

such men, to establish despotism over such a mighty continental *nation*, must be in vain, must be fatal. We shall be *forced ultimately to retract*; let us retract when we can, not when we must.[16]

Pitt's moving speech was revealing and prophetic. Although sixty-eight of his colleagues voted against his motion, eighteen voted for it. Clearly he was not alone; British opinions about British-American problems were as varied and conflicting as those of the American patriots and loyalists. And Pitt had used the word *nation* to describe the American colonies, reflecting a growing recognition in Britain that America possessed sufficient natural and human resources to stand on its own if it so chose. Britain profited and prospered from those abundant colonial resources; for its own good, therefore, rather than risk losing these benefits entirely, it should seek a just and generous reconciliation with America.

Pitt and his followers remained in the minority, however, and the "fatal" and fateful struggle he feared and predicted began only three months later. Following the advice of the Suffolk Resolves, many American colonists had begun arming themselves. In April 1775, the new governor of Massachusetts, General Thomas Gage, learned that patriots had stored a cache of arms in the village of Concord, twenty-one miles west of Boston, and he decided to send troops to destroy these weapons. During the night of April 18, about seven hundred British soldiers set out for Concord. The next morning they found a force of about eighty armed colonial militiamen waiting for them on the Common, or green, of the village of Lexington. The British commander called on the colonials to throw down their weapons; but in the heat of the moment shots rang out (the question of which side fired first remains unanswered), and ten minutes later eight Americans lay dead on the green.

The British arrived at Concord at about 8 A.M. There they skirmished with armed colonials at North Bridge, about a mile from the village green; responding to alarms, militiamen from surrounding towns steadily converged on the area, their numbers eventually swelling to over 4,000. At about noon the British decided to retreat. As they marched along, the militiamen followed, sniping at them almost continuously from behind rocks and trees. By the time they reached Boston, the British counted 73 men killed, 174 wounded, and 26 missing, while the American casualties were 50 killed and 34 wounded. The American War of Independence had begun.

Different Motives and Various Designs

Yet even after blood had been spilled, opinions about what course the colonies should now take remained diverse. "Volumes have been written," radical revolutionary philosopher Thomas Paine wrote in 1776, "on the subject of the struggle between England and America. Men of all ranks have embarked in the controversy, from different motives, and with various designs."[17] Among these ranks were some Americans who simply did not desire independence from Britain. Historian Merrill Jensen explains:

The Battle of Concord proved that colonial militiamen could hold their own against British soldiers.

> Simple loyalty to the mother country was a real if intangible and unweighable force that shaped opinion. Britain was "home" even to some Americans who had never crossed the Atlantic. . . . There was also a loyalty born of the understandable self-interest of officeholders who had achieved status and power within the governmental machinery of the British Empire. . . . Their feeling was shared by many American merchants. They objected to British measures, but they knew that as a part of the empire, Americans belonged to the greatest trading area in the world, and merchants found it difficult to conceive of carrying on trade outside its boundaries.[18]

Another brand of opposition to independence stemmed from the belief that it was foolhardy and suicidal for a small nation of two and a half million people to go to war with the greatest empire on earth. Meanwhile, conservative patriots continued to hope and work for reconciliation with Britain, until the Declaration of Independence finally removed the last possibility of realizing that goal.

By that time even the radicals were divided into factions. Some championed the idea of giving all Americans, even the poorest and least educated, a political voice. Many other revolutionary leaders, though firmly committed to independence and equal rights for all, nevertheless believed that they and other well-to-do aristocrats should run both the Revolution and the new country. They hoped that the war would not bring about a social revolution in which the "mob rule" of the common people would prevail.

Greenhaven Press's *Opposing Viewpoints Digests: The American Revolution* examines these conflicting convictions among loyalists and conservative and radical patriots that divided colonists before and during the Revolutionary War. In chapters 1 through 3, arguments for and against Parliament's right to tax the colonies, debates on declaring independence, and opposing views about the feasibility of winning the war are presented in the first person, in the context of their time, and draw mainly on original speeches, letters, and other documents of that era. The last chapter examines the debate among modern historians about the nature of the Revolution and the divided opinions of its makers. Was the American War of Independence simply a political revolution against British rule, or was it also a social revolution, in which people of all walks of life sought a voice in the new government? Thomas Paine remarked that once the Revolution's first shots had been fired, "the period of debate is closed."[19] Perhaps, if somehow transported to the present, Paine would be surprised to learn that after more than two centuries that debate continues.

1. About half of these refugees went to England, Scotland, and the West Indies (Jamaica, the Bahamas, Bermuda, and other islands), most of the other half to Canada and Nova Scotia.

2. Samuel Eliot Morison, *The Oxford History of the American People*. New York: Oxford University Press, 1965, p. 180.

3. Quoted in Edmund S. Morgan and Helen M. Morgan, *The Stamp Act Crisis: Prologue to Revolution*. Chapel Hill: University of North Carolina Press, 1953, p. 37.

4. Quoted in Morgan and Morgan, *Stamp Act Crisis*, p. 38.

5. Harry M. Ward, *The American Revolution: Nationhood Achieved, 1763–1788*. New York: St. Martin's Press, 1995, pp. 34–35.

6. The actual text of Henry's speech was unfortunately never recorded, so to piece together its major elements historians have had to rely on the fragmentary recollections of various eyewitnesses. Author William Wirt recorded some of these in his 1817 biography of Henry, including interview testimony by Thomas Jefferson, who was present when Henry delivered the speech. "I well remember the cry of treason," Jefferson recalled some fifty-two years after the event, "the pause of Mr. Henry at the name of George the Third, and the presence of mind with which he closed his sentence." (See Samuel Eliot Morison, ed., *Sources and Documents Illustrating the American Revolution, 1764–1788, and the Formation of the Federal Constitution*. Oxford: Clarendon Press, 1953, pp. 16–17.)

7. Quoted in Max Beloff, ed., *The Debate on the American Revolution, 1761–1783*. London: Adam and Charles Black, 1960, p. 71.

8. Quoted in Richard B. Morris, ed., *The American Revolution, 1763–1783: A Bicentennial Collection*. Columbia: University of South Carolina Press, 1970, p. 80.

9. Quoted in Morison, *Sources and Documents*, p. 53.

10. Quoted in Morris, *The American Revolution*, p. 124.

11. Quoted in Henry S. Commager and Richard B. Morris, eds., *The Spirit of 'Seventy-Six: The Story of the American Revolution as Told by Participants*, vol. 1. New York: Bobbs-

Merrill, 1958, p. 39. This spontaneous meeting was technically illegal, since Virginia's governor had only hours before dissolved the Virginia legislature after its members had resolved that the Boston Port Act was a "hostile invasion" of the colonies.

12. Morison, *Oxford History of the American People*, p. 205.

13. Quoted in Morison, *Sources and Documents*, p. 117.

14. Quoted in Commager and Morris, *The Spirit of 'Seventy-Six*, vol. 1, p. 54.

15. *Declaration and Resolves of the First Continental Congress*, in Morison, *Sources and Documents*, pp. 119, 122.

16. Quoted in Beloff, *Debate*, pp. 189–90, 194.

17. Thomas Paine, *Common Sense*, in Beloff, *Debate*, p. 245.

18. Merrill Jensen, *The Founding of a Nation: A History of the American Revolution, 1763–1776*. New York: Oxford University Press, 1968, p. 660.

19. Paine, *Common Sense*, in Beloff, *Debate*, p. 245.

CHAPTER 1

Prewar Disputes

"Why should any Englishman anywhere be exempt from the taxes levied by a legislature made up of Englishmen? Clearly, he should not be exempt, for every member of Parliament represents him in the virtual sense."

Parliament Has the Right to Tax the Colonies

Author's Note: The arguments in the essays in this chapter are stated in the first person and presented in the context of their time, namely the mid-to-late 1760s and early 1770s, when tensions were mounting between Britain and its American colonies.

The American colonies have lately made much ado about the British Parliament taxing them. In particular, they single out the recent Stamp Act, saying first that it is unfair and illegal to tax an Englishman without his consent, and second that it is even more outrageous to tax him when he has no elected representatives in the legislature levying that tax. "No taxation without representation!" is the indignant cry heard with increasing frequency from colonial leaders.

The illogic and indeed utter absurdity of these arguments are relatively easy to demonstrate. First, the idea that a person needs to give consent to be taxed defies both common sense and reality. As the honorable Soame Jenyns, well-known member of

Parliament and the Board of Trade, explains in his recently distributed pamphlet refuting American objections to taxation:

> That no Englishman is or can be taxed but by his own consent . . . is so far from being true, that it is the very reverse of truth; for no man that I know of is taxed by his own consent, and an Englishman, I believe, is as little likely to be so taxed as any man in the world.[1]

The argument that the colonists must have their own representatives in Parliament in order for that body to tax them is equally without foundation. First, the Americans *are* represented in Parliament in the sense that the members of that distinguished legislature work diligently and conscientiously to see to the interests and uphold the rights of all English subjects everywhere, including in America. Thomas Whately, secretary to the distinguished prime minister George Grenville, elaborates in his own recent pamphlet:

> The fact is, that the inhabitants of the colonies are represented in Parliament: they do not indeed choose the members of that assembly; neither are nine tenths of the people of Britain electors. . . . The colonies are in exactly the same situation: All British subjects are really in the same: none are actually, all are virtually represented in Parliament; for every member of Parliament sits in the House [of Commons, one of the two houses of Parliament] not as a representative of his own constituents, but as one of that august assembly by which all the Commons [common people] of Great Britain are represented. Their rights and their interests, however his own borough may be affected by general dispositions, ought to be the great objects of his attentions, and the only rules for his conduct.[2]

Whately's point is well taken. The British towns of Manchester and Birmingham, among the richest and most prosperous in

This Pennsylvania newspaper temporarily ceased publication after the passage of the Stamp Act of 1765.

the kingdom, presently have no directly elected representatives in Parliament. Does this mean that their inhabitants are not Englishmen or that Parliament should exempt them from taxation? Of course not! Why should any Englishman anywhere be exempt from the taxes levied by a legislature made up of Englishmen? Clearly, he should not be exempt, for every member of Parliament represents him in the virtual sense. Mr. Jenyns here argues that this same logic can and must be applied to the American colonies:

Why does not this imaginary [virtual] representation extend to America as well as over the whole island of Great Britain? If it can travel three hundred miles, why not three thousand? If it can jump over rivers and mountains, why cannot it sail over the ocean? If the towns of Manchester and Birmingham, sending no representatives to Parliament, are notwithstanding there represented, why are not the cities of Albany and Boston equally represented in that assembly? Are they not alike British subjects? are they not Englishmen? or are they only Englishmen when they solicit for protection, but not Englishmen when taxes are required to enable this country to protect them?[3]

Mr. Jenyns's last remark, about protection, leads us to another reason why it is both right and just for Parliament to tax its colonies, including its American ones. The American colonial leaders who complain so much now about the Stamp Act and other taxes levied by Parliament appear to have very short memories. Perhaps they need to be reminded that only a few years ago they benefited from Britain's victory in the Seven Years' War.[4] After George Washington and not a few other local military officers were soundly defeated by French and Indian marauders, they wasted little time in appealing for help from the mother country. And Britain not only sent that aid, but also won the war, saved the colonies from destruction, and in gaining new lands ceded by the losers opened up bright new economic opportunities for the colonists. Is it too much to ask now for a bit of gratitude in return? Lord Grenville himself comments on this point:

> Protection and obedience are reciprocal [work both ways]. Great Britain protects America, America is bound to yield obedience. If not, tell me when the Americans were emancipated? When they want the protection of this kingdom, they are always very ready to ask it. That protection has always been afforded them in the most full and ample manner. The nation has run itself into an immense debt to give them this protection; and now they are called upon to contribute a small share towards the public expense.[5]

The question of colonial taxation can be viewed from a different perspective, namely that of the Americans taxing themselves. People on both sides of the ocean have suggested that it would be far more equitable for Parliament to set revenue quotas for each colony; that is, a colony could raise its fair share of the money needed to fund its protection by the mother country by authorizing the legislature of that colony to levy local taxes and send the funds to Parliament. On the positive side, the residents could scarcely complain, since they would now be paying a tax imposed by their own duly elected representatives. On the negative side, however, it is hardly realistic to trust these local legislatures to do their duty to the Crown and raise and send the money. "Have their assemblies shown so much obedience to the Crown," Mr. Jenyns asks, "that we could reasonably expect that they would immediately tax themselves on the arbitrary command of a [British] minister?"[6] The answer is plain. The men presently holding sway in the colonial legislatures, the same men who show so much ingratitude to the sovereign and nation that protects their very lives, cannot be trusted to tax themselves and then hand the money over to Parliament.

In fact, these colonial leaders who are making such fuss and furor over a tax that amounts to only one-third of a day's earnings per year per wage earner should not be thought of as representing the views of most Americans. The average American colonial is a loyal British subject who surely understands and does not object to helping support the mother country that nurtures and protects him. These complainers represent a radical, selfish element that wants to receive and enjoy the many benefits that accrue from being a part of a great empire without giving anything in return. Their supporters are society's lowest order of riffraff and ruffians. This was proven time and again in the recent riots and other incidents of mob violence that occurred in a number of American towns after the imposition of the Stamp Act. Francis Bernard, the upstanding governor of Massachusetts, recalls how his assistant, Thomas

Hutchinson, who had nothing to do with imposing the tax, lost his home, belongings, and very nearly his life to a mindless mob:

> The lieutenant governor . . . being conscious that he had not in the least deserved to be made a party in regard to the Stamp Act . . . rested in full security that the mob would not attack him, and he was at supper with his family when he received advice that the mob were coming to him. He immediately sent away his children, and determined to stay in the house himself, but happily his eldest daughter returned and declared she would not stir from the house unless he went with her; by which means she got him away, which was undoubtedly the occasion of saving his life. For as soon as the mob had got into the house, with a most irresistible fury they immediately looked about for him to murder him. . . . They went to work with a rage scarce to be exemplified by the most savage people. Everything movable was destroyed . . . except such things of value as were worth carrying off.[7]

As a civilized people, we cannot allow a lawless and self-centered minority of colonists to dictate to Parliament what laws it can make or what taxes it can impose. Parliament represents the best interests of all the king's subjects and can and will continue to levy taxes when it deems them in those best interests.

1. Soame Jenyns, *The Objections to the Taxation of Our American Colonies by the Legislature of Great Britain, Briefly Considered*, in Samuel Eliot Morison, ed., *Sources and Documents Illustrating the American Revolution, 1764–1788, and the Formation of the Federal Constitution*. Oxford: Clarendon Press, 1953, p. 19.

2. Thomas Whately, *The Regulations Lately Made Concerning the Colonies and the Taxes Imposed upon Them, Considered*, in Edmund S. Morgan and Helen M. Morgan, *The Stamp Act Crisis: Prologue to Revolution*. Chapel Hill: University of North Carolina Press, 1953, pp. 76–77. The pamphlet was at first anonymous and most Americans assumed that it was the work of Grenville himself, since it clearly reflected his views.

3. Jenyns, *Objections*, in Morison, *Sources and Documents*, p. 20.

4. This was what Europeans called the war fought from 1756 to 1763 between Britain and France (Spain eventually joined France against Britain). The conflict raged in various sectors of the world; in North America, the British colonists referred to it as the French and Indian War because the French enlisted as allies several Indian tribes. At the war's conclusion, Britain acquired Canada from France and Florida from Spain.

5. George Grenville, "Speech to the British House of Commons, January 14, 1766," in Max Beloff, ed., *The Debate on the American Revolution, 1761–1783*. London: Adam and Charles Black, 1960, p. 98.

6. Jenyns, *Objections*, in Morison, *Sources and Documents*, p. 22.

7. "Letter from Governor Francis Bernard to Lord Halifax, August 15, 1765," in William Dudley, ed., *The American Revolution*. San Diego: Greenhaven Press, 1992, p. 44.

"Taxation and representation are inseparable; this position is founded on the laws of nature . . . for whatever is a man's own, is absolutely his own; no man has a right to take it from him without his consent."

Parliament Has No Right to Tax the Colonies

There are two ways in which Parliament might attempt to gain money from the American colonies. The first is indirectly, or "externally," as, for example, through imposing trade regulations. This is perfectly acceptable, for as noted Maryland lawyer Daniel Dulany has pointed out in his recent pamphlet, the mother country's welfare depends in large degree on its transoceanic trade. Therefore, it has the right to regulate such trade through duties on imports and exports, "and if an incidental revenue should be produced by such regulations, these are not . . . unwarrantable."[1]

However, the second way of gaining money from the colonies—through direct, or "internal," taxation—is unacceptable and in fact unethical and illegal. Dulany states, "It appears to me that there is a clear and necessary distinction between an act imposing a tax for *the single purpose of revenue*, and those acts which have been made for the *regulation of trade*, and have produced some revenue in consequence of their effect."[2] This distinction is so obvious that it is clearly recognized by high-placed British ministers as well as by colonists like Dulany. Speaking in Parliament in January 1766 in reply to George Grenville, who as prime minister pushed through the Stamp Act, the respected William Pitt declared: "If the gentleman does not understand the difference between external and internal taxes, I cannot help it; but there is a plain distinction."[3]

The reason that such internal, revenue-producing taxes such as those imposed by the Stamp Act are unacceptable and illegal is that they are levied without the consent of the per-

William Pitt, earl of Chatham, protested Parliament's taxation of the American colonies.

sons being taxed. That consent could be given through their representative in the legislature that levied the tax, if they had such a representative; however, they do not. To pay the tax under these circumstances would make them little better than slaves knuckling under to a master. Once more, we need not rely solely on the colonists to plead their case, for we have instead the testimony of one of Britain's most respected ministers, Lord Camden:

> Taxation and representation are inseparable; this position is founded on the laws of nature; it is more, it is itself an external law of nature; for whatever is a man's own, is absolutely his own; no man has a right to take it from him without his consent, either expressed by himself or [a] representative; whoever attempts to do it, attempts an injury; whoever does it commits a robbery; he throws down and destroys the distinction between liberty and slavery.[4]

Indeed, this right to give consent, via a representative in the legislature, in matters of taxation is one of the fundamental cornerstones of the accumulated laws, decrees, and customs known collectively as the English Constitution. The colonists recognize that they are Englishmen and simply want to avail themselves of their rights as Englishmen. Colonial representative Benjamin Franklin explained this position when questioned recently by the House of Commons. The colonists, he said,

> are entitled to all the privileges and liberties of Englishmen; they find in the great charters, and the petition and declaration of rights [parts of the English Constitution], that one of the privileges of English subjects is, that they are not to be taxed but by their common consent. They have therefore relied upon it, from the first settlement of the province, that the Parliament never would, never could . . . assume a right of taxing them, till it had qualified itself to exercise such right by admitting representatives from the people to be taxed.[5]

Of late, the British have tended to reply to this argument with the supposition that the colonists *are* represented in Parliament, if not in the actual sense, than in the virtual sense; that is, that the members of Parliament are honorable, diligent men who try always to look out for the interests of all British subjects everywhere, even those who are not represented in the legislature in the physical sense. Furthermore, they say, certain British cities have no actual representatives in Parliament and yet do not claim to be exempt from taxes levied by that body.

The Americans Soaked and Gouged

However, this supposition rests on quicksand; or as Mr. Dulany says, "is a mere cob-web, spread to catch the unwary, and entangle the weak";[6] for so-called virtual representation is not real representation. First, the inhabitants of those underrepresented British cities could, at some future date, elect representatives to Parliament; whereas the Americans cannot and will never be able to do so because of the great distance separating the colonies and mother country. The colonists, Mr. Dulany maintains, are "incapable of being electors [in Parliament], the privilege of election being exercisable only in person."[7] To attend Parliament on a regular basis they would have to move to Britain, in which case they would no longer be residents of the colonies.

Second, many members of Parliament have land, relatives, friends, or other tangible connections to the aforementioned British cities. Because of these connections, these members might think twice about levying taxes on underrepresented British cities, since in oppressing those cities they are indirectly hurting themselves. On the other hand, as Dulany puts it:

> There is not the intimate and inseparable relation between the electors of Great Britain and the inhabitants of the colonies, which must inevitably involve both in the same taxation. On the contrary, not a

single actual elector in England might be immediately affected by a taxation in America.[8]

Essentially, this means that such electors can, at their will, as they most certainly have in the case of the Stamp Act, financially soak and gouge the underrepresented Americans with impunity.

Part of the reasoning these members of Parliament use to justify their internal taxation of America is that the colonies owe the mother country a share of the considerable expense of protecting them. "Great Britain protects America, America is bound to yield obedience," Minister Grenville stated recently. "If not, tell me when the Americans were emancipated?"[9] The best possible answer to this flagrantly insensitive question came from Mr. Pitt in his brilliant rebuttal to Grenville's haughty blusterings: "The Gentleman asks when were the colonists emancipated? But I desire to know, when were they made slaves?"[10] Clearly, the colonists are not slaves, but Englishmen, and as such they are beholden to the mother country for its protection, especially during the recent French and Indian War, a conflict that sorely threatened America's well-being.

Yet Minister Grenville needs to realize that the colonists did not sit idly by during the war; in fact, great numbers of Americans fought alongside the British regulars to help the mother country win victory, prestige, and new lands and trade routes. And in doing so at their own expense, the colonists contributed their fair share to the cost of the conflict. Mr. Franklin summed it up well in his interview in the Commons:

Q. Do you think it right that America should be protected by this country and pay no part of the expense?

A. That is not the case. The colonies raised, clothed, and paid during the last war, near 25,000 men and spent many millions.

Q. Were you not reimbursed by Parliament?

A. We were only reimbursed what, in your opinion, we had advanced beyond our proportion, or beyond what might reasonably be expected from us; and it was a very small part of what we spent. Pennsylvania, in particular, disbursed about £500,000, and the reimbursements, in the whole, did not exceed £60,000.[11]

Since Parliament has not reimbursed the colonies all of what it owes them for their war expenses, Britain actually owes the *colonies* for protecting *Britain*, not the other way around.

The plain truth is that the colonies will not pay the stamp tax, nor any other similar internal tax levied by Parliament. When asked in the Commons whether they would pay the stamp tax if it was somehow modified, Franklin answered: "No; they will never submit to it." And when asked if there was any way that the colonists would change their minds about Parliament's right to tax them: "They will never do it, unless compelled by force of arms."[12] We are hopeful that Parliament will see reason and that the present disagreement will never escalate into the need for such force.

1.   Daniel Dulany, *Considerations on the Propriety of Imposing Taxes in the British Colonies, for the Purpose of Raising a Revenue, by Act of Parliament*, in Samuel Eliot Morison, ed., *Sources and Documents Illustrating the American Revolution, 1764–1788, and the Formation of the Federal Constitution*. Oxford: Clarendon Press, 1953, p. 30.

2.   Dulany, *Considerations*, in Morison, *Sources and Documents*, p. 30.

3.   William Pitt, "Speech to the British House of Commons, January 14, 1766," in Max Beloff, ed., *The Debate on the American Revolution, 1761–1783*. London: Adam and Charles Black, 1960, p. 102.

4.   Lord Camden, "Speech to House of Lords on American Taxation, February 24, 1766," in Beloff, *Debate*, p. 121.

5.   "Examination of Benjamin Franklin Before British House of Commons, February 13, 1766," in Richard B. Morris, ed., *The American Revolution, 1763–1783: A Bicentennial Collection*. Columbia: University of South Carolina Press, 1970, p. 85.

6. Dulany, *Considerations*, in Morison, *Sources and Documents*, p. 26.

7. Dulany, *Considerations*, in Morison, *Sources and Documents*, p. 27.

8. Dulany, *Considerations*, in Morison, *Sources and Documents*, p. 27.

9. George Grenville, "Speech to the British House of Commons, January 14, 1766," in Beloff, *Debate*, p. 98.

10. Pitt, "Speech of January 14, 1766," in Beloff, *Debate*, p. 102.

11. "Examination of Benjamin Franklin," in Morris, *American Revolution*, p. 82.

12. "Examination of Benjamin Franklin," in Morris, *American Revolution*, pp. 84, 86.

"The same power that can take away our right of electing councilors by our representatives can take away from the other colonies the right of choosing even representatives."

Parliament Is Abusing American Rights

The British Parliament is lately guilty of several clear-cut abuses of the American colonists' rights as Englishmen. Among the most serious of these transgressions is a breach of both the content and spirit of the charters granted to the colonies by the Crown on the occasions of their foundings. These charters are very much legal contracts. Their language makes it clear that the colonies agreed to remain loyal subjects, subordinate to and dependent on the mother country; and in return the British government promised to protect them and grant them all of the rights and privileges of free Englishmen. "This is abundantly proved," states former Rhode Island governor Stephen Hopkins in his recent pamphlet titled *The Rights of Colonies Examined,*

> by the charter given to the Massachusetts colony, while they were still in England, and which they received and brought over with them. . . . The colonies of Connecticut and Rhode Island, also, afterwards obtained charters from the Crown, granting them the like ample privileges. By all these charters, it is in the most express and solemn manner granted, that these adventurers, and their chil-

44

dren after them forever, should have and enjoy all the freedom and liberty that the subjects in England enjoy; that they might make laws for their own government . . . agreeable to the laws of England; that they might purchase lands, acquire goods and use trade for their advantage, and have an absolute property in whatever they justly acquired. These, with many other gracious privileges, were granted them by several kings; and they were to pay, as an acknowledgment to the Crown, only one-fifth part of the ore of gold and silver, that should at any time be found in said colonies, in lieu of, and full satisfaction for, all dues and demands of the Crown and king of England upon them.[1]

There is nothing unusual about these agreements and arrangements made with the American colonies; indeed, other British colonies in diverse parts of the globe have received similar charters and grants of rights.

Yet the Government Act, one of the pernicious Intolerable Acts passed by Parliament to punish Boston for its famous "tea party," has permanently altered the charter granted Massachusetts in 1691. The act provides for the colony's council, previously elected by the lower house of the local legislature and approved by the colonial governor, to be appointed by the king. Also, the local governor, the king's crony, has been given the power to appoint local judges without the consent of the council; and local town meetings, long vital arenas in which individual colonists express their concerns about legal and political matters, can now be held only once a year unless special permission is obtained from the governor. Boston's Dr. Joseph Warren, an upstanding and respected local patriot, voiced our concerns in a recent letter to his distinguished colleague, Mr. John Adams:

> It is not simply the appointment of the Council by the King that we complain of; it is the breach thereby made in our charter; and, if we suffer this, none

of our charter-rights are worth naming; the charters of all the colonies are no more than blank paper. The same power that can take away our right of electing councilors by our representatives can take away from the other colonies the right of choosing even representatives.[2]

Another abuse of colonial rights involves the ominous presence of the British military in our cities and towns. The first Quartering Act (also known as the Mutiny Act), passed by Parliament in 1765, authorized colonial governors to open up various buildings for the use of British regulars. Much more intrusive is the more recent Quartering Act, another of the Intolerable Acts, a measure supposedly directed only against Bostonians, but in reality a potential lethal threat to all American colonists. The act allows British troops to be quartered in local homes and other buildings when no barracks are available to them.

The presence of these troops, obviously designed to intimidate the colonists into blind obedience to the Crown, could lead to more of the kind of needless bloodshed that, as everyone knows, occurred in March 1770. At that time two regiments of British soldiers were quartered in Boston under the guise of protecting British officials executing the Customs Acts. Some of the details of this "Boston Massacre" were recounted by the *Boston Gazette* on March 12, a week after the incident:

> Thirty or forty persons, mostly lads . . . [had] gathered in King Street, [when] Capt. Preston [a British officer] with a party of men with charged bayonets, came [at them] . . . pushing their bayonets, [and] crying make way! . . . Continuing to push to drive the people off, [they] pricked some in several places. . . . [The crowd retaliated by throwing] snow balls. On this, the Captain commanded them to fire. . . . The soldiers continued to fire successively till seven or eight or, as some say, eleven guns were discharged.

Paul Revere's 1770 engraving depicts British soldiers firing on defenseless Americans during the Boston Massacre.

> By this fatal maneuver three men were laid dead on the spot and two more struggling for life; but what showed a degree of cruelty unknown to British troops . . . was an attempt to fire upon or push with their bayonets the persons who undertook to remove the slain and wounded![3]

The final death toll of these innocents was five, with several others wounded. Equally outrageous was the result of the soldiers' trial: Captain Preston was acquitted and two of the soldiers received mild sentences for manslaughter. The continued quartering of British troops in Massachusetts and other colonies only increases the risk that such horrendous events will be repeated, perhaps on an even larger scale.

Still other abuses have occurred. Some of these were listed by Samuel Adams in the 1772 *Proceedings of the Town of Boston:*

> The British . . . have assumed the power of legisla-
> tion for the colonists in all cases whatever, without
> obtaining the consent of the inhabitants. . . . They
> have asserted that assumed power, in raising a rev-
> enue in the colonies without their consent. . . . A
> number of new officers, unknown in the charter of
> this province, have been appointed to superintend
> this revenue. . . . These officers are by their com-
> mission invested with powers altogether unconstitu-
> tional, and entirely destructive to that security which
> we have a right to enjoy. . . . Thus our houses and
> even our bed chambers are exposed to be ransacked,
> our boxes, chests, and trunks broken open, ravaged
> and plundered by wretches, whom no prudent man
> would venture to employ even as menial servants.[4]

Parliament apparently assumes that it has unlimited power to abuse the American colonies by denying them the rights granted them not only by prior charters and promises, but also by natural law. A higher power limits the authority of Britain's legislature, a power to whom it, the colonies, and people everywhere must ultimately answer. As Boston lawyer James Otis phrased it in his widely read 1764 pamphlet:

> To say that Parliament is absolute . . . is a contradic-
> tion. . . . Parliaments are in all cases to declare what
> is for the good of the whole; but it is not the decla-
> ration of Parliament that makes it so. There must be
> in every instance a higher authority . . . God. Should
> an act of Parliament be against any of His natural
> laws, which are immutably true, their declaration
> would be contrary to eternal truth, equity, and jus-
> tice, and consequently void.[5]

1. Stephen Hopkins, *The Rights of Colonies Examined*, in William Dudley, ed., *The American Revolution*. San Diego: Greenhaven Press, 1992, pp. 56–57.

2. "Letter from Dr. Joseph Warren to John Adams, August 15, 1774," quoted in David Ammerman, *In Common Cause: American Response to the Coercive Acts of 1774*. Charlottesville: University Press of Virginia, 1974, p. 8.

3. "The Boston Massacre, March 5, 1770," *Boston Gazette*, in Richard B. Morris, ed., *The American Revolution, 1763–1783: A Bicentennial Collection*. Columbia: University of South Carolina Press, 1970, p. 107.

4. "List of Infringements and Violations of Rights," *Proceedings of the Town of Boston, October–November 1772*, in Samuel Eliot Morison, ed., *Sources and Documents Illustrating the American Revolution, 1764–1788, and the Formation of the Federal Constitution*. Oxford: Clarendon Press, 1953, pp. 91–92.

5. James Otis, *The Rights of British Colonies Asserted and Proved*, in Morison, *Sources and Documents*, p. 7.

"Each colony signed an agreement and thereby became a British corporation subject to certain rules, among them the right of Parliament to regulate and tax it. It is both illegal and irresponsible for any such colony/corporation now to claim it is not bound to follow the rules to which it willingly agreed."

Parliament Is Not Abusing American Rights

The charge that Parliament is abusing the rights of American colonists is based on a false supposition, one that, unfortunately, an increasing number of colonists have blindly come to accept of late. According to this supposition, Americans are endowed with all the various rights enjoyed by citizens of the mother country. However, a sober examination of the facts demonstrates plainly that this is not the case. The confusion apparently derives from equating personal rights and political rights, which in reality have different natures and sources.

Consider first our personal rights, including life, liberty, and property. These are our birthright as Englishmen, granted us by common law accumulated through the centuries, and are, in fact, the birthright of all Englishmen, whether born in Britain or one of its colonies. Thus, no governmental power, be it king, Parliament, or local governor or assembly, can enslave us, imprison us, or confiscate our property arbitrarily or without due process of English law. These, then, are the rights we have in common with the citizens of the mother country.

By contrast, the political rights of British colonists are not derived directly from common law. Instead, the original charters of the colonies define and place limitations on such rights and privileges, including the right of local assemblies to make laws or claim exemption from the acts and laws passed by Parliament. As Sir Francis Bernard, governor of Massachusetts from 1760 to 1769, stated in a letter to his colleague, Lord Barrington, "In Britain the American governments [local legislatures] are considered as corporations empowered to make by-laws, existing only during the pleasure of Parliament . . . [which has] at any time a power to dissolve them."[1] Martin Howard, a distinguished lawyer from Newport, Rhode Island, elaborated on this principle in his recent pamphlet:

> The political rights of the colonies or the powers of government communicated to them are more limited, and their nature, quality, and extent depend altogether upon the patent or charter which first created and instituted them. As individuals, the colonists participate of every blessing the English constitution can give them: as corporations created by the Crown, they are confined within the primitive [specific and limiting] views of their institution. Whether, therefore, their indulgence is scanty or liberal can be no cause of complaint; for when they accepted of their charters they tacitly submitted to the terms and conditions of them. The colonies have no rights independent of their charters; they can claim no greater than those give them; by those the Parliamentary jurisdiction over them is not taken away.[2]

In other words, each colony signed an agreement and thereby became a British corporation subject to certain rules, among them the right of Parliament to regulate and tax it. It is both illegal and irresponsible for any such colony/corporation now to claim it is not bound to follow the rules to which it willingly agreed. And therefore, Parliament's regulation of trade, imposition of certain mild taxes, and local quartering of troops to protect and maintain order within the colonies are not abuses of the colonists' personal rights.

Chief among these so-called abuses is Parliament's imposition of taxes "without the people's consent" or "without representation in Parliament." This complaint is groundless, for all Englishmen are well represented by the members of Parliament. As Mr. Howard states, these members "are the representatives of every British subject, wheresoever he be,"[3] even of those subjects who cannot vote for them. Many residents of Britain cannot vote, for example, among them some of the realm's wealthiest and most socially influential citizens. Yet, these people do not whine about abuses of their rights, but instead cheerfully submit to the will of the well-meaning and admirably qualified legislators who look after the nation's interests.

And even if this utopian privilege of direct representation was extended to the colonies, what would be accomplished? A handful of American members of Parliament would have no power to outvote the majority on important issues. "In short," Mr. Howard contends, "this right of representation is but a phantom, and if possessed in its full extent would be of no real advantage to the colonies."[4]

Yet if one is looking for examples of abuses of rights, there is no need to waste words with these hypothetical and philosophical arguments. I speak now not of Parliament's abuses of American rights, which have been shown to be nonexistent, but of the colonists' own blatant abuses of a wide variety of rights and privileges. The wanton destruction of a valuable shipment of tea by a lawless mob of Bostonians is a prime example. During the debate in Parliament that followed this travesty, Frederick Lord North, the British prime minister, summarized other similar abuses and called on his colleagues to do something about them:

The Americans have tarred and feathered [our] subjects, plundered [our] merchants, burnt [our] ships, denied all obedience to [our] laws and authority; yet so clement and so long forbearing has our conduct been that it is incumbent on us now to take a different course. . . . The measure now proposed [the Government Act, one of the Coercive Acts] is nothing more than taking the election of councilors out of the hands of those people who are continually acting in defiance and resistance of [our] laws.[5]

Rebellious Bostonians demonstrate their unhappiness with Parliament's taxes by tarring and feathering British subjects.

Indeed, how can those who repeatedly defy the law expect to be taken seriously when they complain of abuses? An irate colonist, one of the majority who remain loyal and law-abiding British subjects, responded to the Boston tea incident in a letter printed in the *Massachusetts Gazette*:

> Whenever a factious set of people rise to such a pitch of insolence, as to prevent the execution of the laws, or destroy the property of individuals, just as their caprice and humor leads them; there is an end of all order and government, riot and confusion must be the natural consequence of such measures. It is impossible for trade to flourish where property is insecure.[6]

The letter writer mentions "a factious set of people" threatening property and the execution of law; indeed, there can be little doubt that such abuses *by*, rather than *of*, the colonists are the work of a small group of troublemakers. Reverend Henry Caner, rector of King's Chapel in Boston, stated it well when he wrote that "sedition, anarchy, and violence" are kept alive in Massachusetts "by about half a dozen men of bad principles and morals."[7] They call themselves the Sons of Liberty, yet their actions threaten the liberty of all the colonists. A recent piece in a New York newspaper was right on the mark in declaring that

> the Sons of Liberty consist of but two sorts of men. The first are those who by their . . . ill conduct in life, are reduced almost to poverty, and are happy in finding a subsistence, though it is even on the destruction of their country; for on the turbulence of the times, and the heated imaginations of the populace, depends their existence. The latter are the ministers of the gospel, who, instead of preaching to their flocks meekness, sobriety, attention to their different employments and a steady obedience to the laws of Britain, belch from the pulpit . . . a steady [stream of propaganda urging people] to shake off their allegiance to the mother country.[8]

Worst of all are the delegates to the so-called Continental Congress, who arrogantly claim to speak for all American colonists. As the author of a recent loyalist pamphlet states, "A very great part of the Americans are not their constituents in any sense at all, as they never voted for them," nor authorized them to act "in the name of the colonies."[9] These same delegates complain that Parliament does not fairly represent them; yet they do not fairly represent the majority of their fellow colonists. In enumerating abuses of rights, these self-styled "patriots" should begin with their own.

1.   Sir Francis Bernard, "Letter to Lord Barrington, November 23, 1765," in Max Beloff, ed., *The Debate on the American Revolution, 1761–1783*. London: Adam and Charles Black, 1960, p. 86.

2.   Martin Howard, *A Letter from a Gentleman at Halifax, to His Friend in Rhode Island, Containing Remarks upon a Pamphlet Entitled the Rights of the Colonies Examined*, in William Dudley, ed., *The American Revolution*. San Diego: Greenhaven Press, 1992, p. 68. This pamphlet, meant as a rebuttal to Stephen Hopkins's *The Rights of the Colonies Examined*, was published anonymously, supposedly by a resident of Halifax, Nova Scotia. In reality, Howard was a resident of Rhode Island and Hopkins's frequent political opponent.

3.   Howard, *Letter from a Gentleman*, in Dudley, *The American Revolution*, p. 71.

4.   Howard, *Letter from a Gentleman*, in Dudley, *The American Revolution*, p. 72.

5.   Lord North, from the debate on a bill regulating the government of the Massachusetts colony, April 22, 1774, quoted in Henry S. Commager and Richard B. Morris, eds., *The Spirit of 'Seventy-Six: The Story of the American Revolution as Told by Participants*, vol. 1. New York: Bobbs-Merrill, 1958, pp. 13–14.

6.   *Massachusetts Gazette, and Boston News-Letter*, November 17, 1774, quoted in Philip Davidson, *Propaganda and the American Revolution, 1763–1783*. New York: W. W. Norton, 1973, pp. 274–75.

7.   Henry Caner, "Letter to Governor Wentworth, November 8, 1773," in Catherine S. Crary, ed., *The Price of Loyalty: Tory Writings from the Revolutionary Era*. New York: McGraw-Hill, 1973, p. 19.

8.   *New York Gazetteer*, March 9, 1775, quoted in Davidson, *Propaganda*, pp. 295–96.

9.   Anonymous, *What Think Ye of Congress Now?* quoted in Davidson, *Propaganda*, pp. 273–74.

CHAPTER 2

Patriotic Versus Loyalist Views

"If we are independent, this land of liberty will be glorious on many accounts. . . . America [will] be an asylum for all noble spirits and sons of liberty from all parts of the world."

America Should Declare Independence from Britain

Author's Note: The arguments in the essays in this chapter are stated in the first person and presented in the context of their time, namely the mid-1770s, when Britain's American colonies seriously began to debate breaking away from the mother country.

British abuses and oppression of the American colonies have escalated to the point of no return. For reasons of both honor and practicality, the colonies should abandon efforts toward reconciliation and immediately declare their independence from the mother country. Since the early 1760s, Parliament and the Crown have initiated one crisis after another, each seemingly more insulting and destructive of colonial interests than the last. The Stamp Act of 1765, which dared to tax us without our consent, was the first serious breach of trust between the two peoples. Parliament wisely repealed it in the following year, for which His Majesty's American subjects were genuinely grateful; but there then followed the Townshend duties, the Boston Massacre, the Tea Act, the repressive Coercive Acts designed to cripple Boston, and most recently, the out-and-out murder of innocent colonists at Concord and Lexington on April 19, 1775. This last, most naked aggression against us was the last straw. The recent, very apt expression of outrage by the citizens of Malden, Massachusetts, is but one of many such statements by colonial towns now demanding a declaration of independence:

> It is now the ardent wish of our souls that America may become a free and independent state. . . . [The final insult came on] the ever memorable nineteenth of April. We remember the fatal day! The expiring groans of our countrymen yet vibrate on our ears! . . . We hear their blood crying to us from the ground for vengeance! . . . The cries of the widow and the orphan demand our attention; they demand that the hand of pity should wipe the tear from their eye, and that the sword of their country should avenge their wrongs. . . . We therefore renounce with disdain our connection with a kingdom of slaves; we bid final adieu to Britain.[1]

Insults, abuses, betrayal, aggression, and bloodshed, then, amply justify the growing American desire to separate from Britain. Ten years ago, five years ago, nay, only two years ago, most colonists would have seen such a course of action as uncertain, foolhardy, self-destructive, and unthinkable. Yet now that the fateful decision is upon us, we cannot help but recognize that we will be better off for doing it; for independence will bring us certain benefits, both immediate and long-term. John Adams, that tireless patriot from Massachusetts, lately recounted the immediate ones:

> The advantages which will result from such a declaration are, in my opinion, very numerous and very great. After that event the colonies will hesitate no longer to complete their governments. . . . The presses will produce no more seditious or traitorous

speculations. Slanders upon public men . . . will be lessened. The legislatures of the colonies will exert themselves to manufacture saltpeter, sulfur, powder, arms, cannon, mortars, clothing, and everything necessary for the support of life. Our civil governments will feel a vigor hitherto unknown. . . . Foreigners will then exert themselves to supply us with what we want. A foreign court will not disdain to treat us upon equal terms. Nay . . . such a declaration, instead of uniting the people of Great Britain against us, will raise such a storm against the measures of administration as will obstruct the war, and throw the kingdom into confusion.[2]

Regarding the long-term benefits of independence, there is first the fact that Americans will be able to decide their own fate. No longer will American legislators, merchants, and landowners wriggle helplessly under the thumbs of Parliament and the king. Indeed, we have no need or use for a king in this virgin, untainted land, which is so far removed from the ancient hatreds, feuds, and other corruptions of the European monarchies. "We can never be willingly subject," state the citizens of Malden, "to any other King than He who, being possessed of infinite wisdom, goodness and rectitude, is alone fit to possess unlimited power."[3] In other words, we say that the only power we should feel obliged to recognize above ourselves is God Almighty!

American independence will also forever put an end to the threat and reality of taxation without representation. And as a nation unto itself, America will no longer be bound to support British wars and alliances, but instead will have the right to pick and choose the nations with whom it wishes to be friends. In a recent pamphlet circulated widely through the colonies, Jacob Green of New Jersey lists other advantages of separating from Britain:

If we are independent, this land of liberty will be glorious on many accounts: Population will abundantly increase, agriculture will be promoted, trade will flourish, religion, unrestrained by human laws, will have free course to run and prevail, and America [will] be an asylum for all noble spirits and sons of liberty from all parts of the world. Hither they may retire from every land of oppression; here they may expand and exult; here they may enjoy all the blessings which this . . . globe [the earth] can afford to fallen men.[4]

Finally, it is essential that we Americans declare our independence *now*, rather than delay and end up saddling our children or grandchildren with the task. For make no mistake about it: An independent America is inevitable! The loyalists among us gasp at such talk, call it treason and insist that we should remain under the mother country's wing. They fail to see the plain truth that Britain is too far away and too detached from our interests to rule us effectively any longer. This is a simple matter of *common sense*, as laid down in the admirable pamphlet penned by one of the most patriotic of all Americans, Tom Paine. "Since nothing but blows will do," he says,

for God's sake, let us come to a final separation, and not leave the next generation to be cutting throats, under the violated unmeaning names of parent and child. . . . As to government matters, it is not in the power of Britain to do this continent justice: The business of it will soon be too weighty, and intricate, to be managed with any tolerable degree of convenience, by a power so distant from us, and so very ignorant of us. . . . To be always running three or four thousand miles with a tale or a petition, waiting four or five months for an answer, which when obtained requires five or six more to explain it in, will in a few years be looked upon as folly and childishness. There was a time when it was proper, and there is a proper time for it to cease. Small islands, not capable of protecting themselves, are the proper

COMMON SENSE;

ADDRESSED TO THE

INHABITANTS

O F

A M E R I C A,

On the following interesting

S U B J E C T S.

I. Of the Origin and Design of Government in general, with concise Remarks on the English Constitution.

II. Of Monarchy and Hereditary Succession.

III. Thoughts on the present State of American Affairs.

IV. Of the present Ability of America, with some miscellaneous Reflections.

Man knows no Master save creating HEAVEN,
Or those whom choice and common good ordain.

THOMSON.

PHILADELPHIA;

Printed, and Sold, by R. BELL, in Third-Street.

MDCCLXXVI.

Thomas Paine argues for the separation of America and Britain in his convincing pamphlet Common Sense.

objects for kingdoms to take under their care; but there is something very absurd in supposing a continent to be perpetually governed by an island. In no instance has nature made the satellite larger than its primary planet, and as England and America, with respect to each other, reverse the common order of nature, it is evident they belong to different systems; England to Europe, America to itself.[5]

For these several reasons, America must be free and independent, a noble goal the people of Malden, like many other Americans, have pledged to seek, support, and defend "to the last drop of their blood, and the last farthing of their treasure."[6]

1. "Declaration of the Citizens of Malden, Massachusetts, May 27, 1776," in Alden T. Vaughan, ed., *Chronicles of the Revolution*. New York: Grosset and Dunlap, 1965, p. 239.

2. John Adams, "Letter to John Winthrop, June 23, 1776," in William Dudley, ed., *The American Revolution*. San Diego: Greenhaven Press, 1992, p. 130.

3. "Declaration of the Citizens of Malden," in Vaughan, *Chronicles*, p. 240.

4. Jacob Green, *Observations on the Reconciliation of Great-Britain and the Colonies*, in Dudley, *The American Revolution*, p. 146.

5. Thomas Paine, *Common Sense*, in Max Beloff, ed., *The Debate on the American Revolution, 1761–1783*. London: Adam and Charles Black, 1960, pp. 252–53.

6. "Declaration of the Citizens of Malden," in Vaughan, *Chronicles*, p. 240.

"The proper course of action is twofold: first, to remain steadfastly loyal to our land of origin and offer no support whatever to the lawless agitators among us; and second, to seek reconciliation with the mother country."

America Should Not Declare Independence from Britain

Under no circumstances should the American colonies declare independence from the mother country. Instead, we should reconcile our differences with and remain loyal to the land that brought us into existence, nurtured us, and continues to protect us from hostile forces at large in the world. Those who call themselves patriots say that the differences between Britain and the colonies have grown so great that there is no longer a chance for reconciliation. But these agitators, for that term fits them better than patriots, do not speak for all the colonists. In fact the agitators represent but a small minority of the population and an exceedingly disreputable one at that. They claim to champion liberty and justice for all; but the reality is that they want to eliminate British rule simply to clear the way so that *they* can rule; and such an administration will surely be a corrupt despotism. Massachusetts lawyer Daniel Leonard was correct in his statement (in an essay published early in 1775) that "the small seed of sedition" that had taken root in the colonies in prior years has grown into "a great tree; the vilest reptiles that crawl upon the earth are concealed at the root; the foulest birds of the air rest upon its branches."[1]

The proof that these agitators are not really supporters of liberty is their disgraceful treatment of their fellow colonists whose sole offense is to disagree with them. They have formed local committees whose members spy on those decent folk who remain loyal to the mother country; and many such loyalists have been denounced for "speaking words inimical [hostile] to the cause of America," while some have been threatened or even physically attacked. In October 1775, the so-called Continental Congress (which, it must be stressed, does *not* represent the majority of colonists) went so far as to order the arrest of anyone its leaders viewed as "dangerous" to their cause. Beset by these outrages, many law-abiding colonists have opted to leave America altogether rather than to live under such a state of fear and tyranny.

But running away is not the answer. The proper course of action is twofold: first, to remain steadfastly loyal to our land of origin and offer no support whatever to the lawless agitators among us; and second, to seek reconciliation with the mother country, which increasingly, and very mistakenly, assumes that the agitators speak for most Americans. In efforts to demonstrate their loyalty to the British, a number of towns and counties have tendered petitions and statements to their local governors or to officials in Britain. A typical example was that of March 10, 1775, by the people of Anson County, North Carolina, which stated in part:

> Permit us, in behalf of ourselves, and many others of His Majesty's most dutiful and loyal subjects . . . [to express] our abomination of the many outrageous attempts now forming on this side of the Atlantic, against the peace and tranquillity of His Majesty's dominions in North America. . . . We are truly sensible that those invaluable blessings which we have hitherto enjoyed under His Majesty's auspicious gov-

ernment, can only be secured to us by the stability of
his throne, supported and defended by the British
Parliament, the only grand bulwark and guardian of
our civil and religious liberties. . . . We are determined, by the assistance of Almighty God . . . steadfastly to continue His Majesty's loyal subjects, and to
contribute all in our power for the preservation of
the public peace; so that, by our unanimous example,
we hope to discourage the desperate endeavors of a
deluded multitude, and to see a misled people turn
again from their atrocious offenses to a proper exercise of their obedience and duty.[2]

Loyalty to the mother country, though first in importance,
is not the only reason for refraining from a split with Britain,
there being practical reasons as well. The British have, it is
true, made their own share of mistakes and caused a certain
amount of ill will and havoc in the colonies in recent years.
But these mistakes and the relatively small harm done in consequence does not warrant a split between parent and child,
and our differences can easily be reconciled by calm discussion and negotiation.

The advantages of such reconciliation are obvious and many.
First, no more lives would be lost needlessly in altercations
such as those at Lexington and Concord. Second, as Charles
Inglis, respected clergyman of New York, tells us in his recent
pamphlet, "By a connection with Great Britain, our trade
would still have the protection of the greatest naval power in
the world." As Inglis points out, "The protection of our trade,
while connected with Britain, will not cost us a *fiftieth* part of
what it must cost were we ourselves to raise a naval force sufficient for the purpose."[3] Moreover, as Inglis and many others
have pointed out, once we have reconciled with the mother
country, within a few years conditions will return to normal
and immigrants will again begin to arrive from different parts
of Europe, swelling our local populations, raising the values of
our lands, and increasing prosperity overall.

Another reason for maintaining our ties with Britain, according to Mr. Inglis, is that the American colonists are Englishmen by temperament and tradition, and therefore are not suited to assuming a new identity and ruling themselves under a democratic form of government. Moreover, they lack the money and resources to do so. "The Americans are properly Britons," says Inglis:

> They have the manners, habits, and ideas of Britons; and have been accustomed to a similar form of government. . . . Besides the unsuitableness of the republican form [of government] to the genius of the people, America is too extensive for it. That form may do well enough for a single city or small territory, but would be utterly improper for such a continent as this. America is too unwieldy for the feeble, dilatory administration of democracy. . . . It is well known that wages and the price of labor, in general, are much higher in America than in England. Labor must necessarily be dear [a precious commodity] in every country where land is cheap and large tracts of it unsettled, as is the case here. . . . Where the money is to come from which will defray this enormous annual expense of [running an independent nation] . . . I know not. . . . What then must our situation be, or what the state of our trade, when oppressed with such a burden of annual expense! When every article of commerce, every necessary of life, together with our lands, must be heavily taxed to defray that expense![4]

If independence be the wrong course for the colonies to take, and reconciliation with Britain the right course, how can such a reconciliation be accomplished? The answer is to strike a compromise with the British that addresses the complaints and needs of both. In a nutshell, the Americans should agree to continue under British rule and protection and to refrain from aggressive, seditious behavior; and in return, Parliament

should agree to address the American grievances that initiated the conflict and guarantee the colonists all rights enjoyed
by Englishmen living in England. New York's Peter Van
Schaack has expressed this position admirably:

> I consider the colonies as members of the British
> Empire, and subordinate to Parliament. . . . At the
> same time, I foresee the destructive consequences of
> a right in Parliament to bind us in all cases whatso-
> ever. To obviate the effects of either extreme, some
> middle way should be found out, by which the ben-
> efits to the Empire should be secured arising from
> the doctrine of a supreme power, while the abuses of
> that power to the prejudices of the colonists should
> be guarded against; and this, I hope, will be the
> happy effect of the present struggle. . . . Absolute
> *dependence* and *independence* are two extremes which I
> would avoid.[5]

1. Quoted in Harry M. Ward, *The American Revolution: Nationhood Achieved, 1763–1788.*
    New York: St. Martin's Press, 1995, p. 260.

2. "Address of the Inhabitants of Anson County, North Carolina, to Governor Josiah
    Martin, March 10, 1775," in Richard B. Morris, ed., *The American Revolution, 1763–
    1783: A Bicentennial Collection.* Columbia: University of South Carolina Press, 1970, pp.
    213, 215.

3. Charles Inglis, *The True Interest of America Impartially Stated, in Certain Strictures on a
    Pamphlet Intitled Common Sense,* in William Dudley, ed., *The American Revolution.* San
    Diego: Greenhaven Press, 1992, pp. 151–52.

4. Inglis, *The True Interest of America,* in Dudley, *The American Revolution,* pp. 155–57.

5. Peter Van Schaack, *Journal,* January 1776, in Morris, *American Revolution,* pp. 206–208.

CHAPTER 3

Wartime Concerns

"We are rushing into a war with our parent state without offering the least concession; without even deigning to propose an accommodation."

A War Against Britain Is Unjustified

Author's Note: The arguments in the essays in this chapter are stated in the first person and presented in the context of their time, mainly the year 1776. Fighting between Britain and its American colonies had already commenced and debate raged among the colonists over whether or not the war should continue.

It is both sad and horrifying to think that these colonies should engage in open warfare with their mother country. Surely we will not risk our great blessings of property, liberty, and tranquil life for the chaos and bloodshed of war. And a *civil* war at that! For what else can one call it when former friends and neighbors find themselves in opposing camps and loyal British subjects are forced to choose between their mother country and the hotheaded cause of the most extreme minded residents of the colonies? Indeed, *extreme* and *rash* are the most fitting words to describe their views and actions; they clamor for war without having made enough of an effort to redress the colonies' complaints against the British, some of which, admittedly, are justified. But justified or not, fighting is the wrong course. In this tract from his *Letters of a Westchester Farmer*, the Reverend Samuel Seabury outlines the right course:

When disputes happen between nations independent of each other, they first attempt to settle them by their ambassadors; they seldom run hastily to war till they have tried what can be done by treaty and mediation. I would make many more concessions to a parent than were justly due to him, rather than engage with him in a duel. But we are rushing into a war with our parent state without offering the least concession; without even deigning to propose an accommodation.[1]

Is not such accommodation better than death and destruction? Are some paltry disagreements over taxes and lost tea worth the loss of life, home, family, and all hope of happiness? For God's sake, consider how beautiful and bounteous these

Public notices like this one were posted throughout the colonies urging people to enlist in the fight for freedom from Britain.

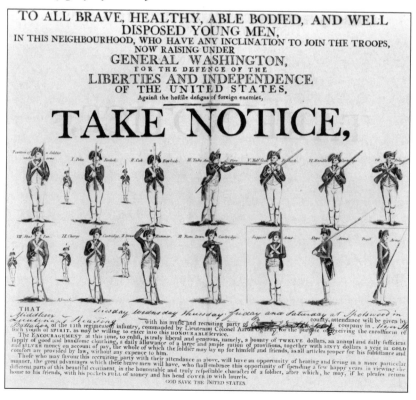

American lands are, the freedom afforded by British laws, and the comfortable lives both have afforded us thus far. By continuing with this unjustified conflict, we will be throwing away our hard work, happy lives, and dreams of a better future. Businessman Joel Stone, of Washington, Connecticut, has aptly voiced this sentiment:

> By dint of an unwearied diligence and a close application to trade I found the number of my friends and customers daily increasing and a fair prospect of long happiness arose to my sanguine mind in one of the most desirable situations beneath the best of laws and the most excellent government in the universe. But, alas, the dreadful commotion [of revolution has] quickly involved that once happy country in all the dreadful horrors of an unnatural war and filling the pleasant land with desolation and blood removed all my fair prospects of future blessings.[2]

The war has already ruined Mr. Stone's life and the lives of many other poor souls, and if it continues it will surely bring misery to us all. And that misery may well take other forms besides the loss of business, property, and livelihood. Meeting recently in Philadelphia, the Quakers, who nobly stand steadfastly against resorting to violence for any reason, called upon all colonists to act reasonably in this crisis. Like Reverend Seabury, they advocated a course of reconciliation with Britain. Further, they warned that proceeding in this rash course of revolution and war could cost the colonists their souls, rightly pointing out that Christ, who "came not to destroy men's lives, but to save them," will surely frown on any who wantonly shed their neighbors' blood:

> We cannot but, with distressed minds, beseech all . . . in the most solemn and awful manner, to consider that, if by their acting and persisting in a proud, selfish spirit, and not regarding the dictates of true wisdom, such measures are pursued as tend to the

shedding of innocent blood; in the day when they
and all men shall appear at the judgment-seat of
Christ, to receive a reward according to their works,
they will be excluded from his favor, and their portion will be in everlasting misery.[3]

If these aforementioned arguments against prosecuting this
unnatural war are not enough to convince any decent person,
then consider another. The small band of men leading the
rebels, who mistakenly call themselves patriots, are the dregs
of society. Does it make sense to throw away our lands, families, and futures to follow the words and actions of such disreputable characters? One very reputable character who
thinks not is Jacob Duché, rector of Christ Church in
Philadelphia. Jacob originally accepted the post of chaplain of
the Continental Congress in hopes of making sure its members brought no harm to colonial churches and their ministers. After just three months, however, he resigned, disgusted
at discovering firsthand the low and destructive designs and
characters of rebel leaders. With an uneasy conscience, he
subsequently wrote to General George Washington, whom he
regarded as one of the few reputable gentlemen in the ranks
of those protesting British policies. "The most respectable
characters have withdrawn themselves [from the rebellion],"
Jacob warned,

> and are succeeded by a great majority of illiberal and
> violent men. . . . O my dear sir! What a sad contrast?
> Characters now present themselves whose minds
> can never mingle with your own. . . . Some of them
> are so obscure that their very names never met my
> ears before, and others have only been distinguished
> for the weakness of their understandings and the
> violence of their tempers. From the New England
> provinces, can you find one that, as a gentleman, you
> could wish to associate with? . . . [They are mainly]
> bankrupts, attorneys and men of desperate fortunes.
> . . . Are the dregs of a Congress then still to influ-

ence a mind like yours? These are not the men you engaged to serve. These are not the men that America has chosen to represent her. . . . With that prudence and delicacy therefore of which I know you to be possessed, represent to Congress the indispensable necessity of rescinding [taking back] the hasty and ill-advised Declaration of Independence.[4]

If we do indeed take back that declaration, composed in the heat of the moment by violent, unthinking men, all will not be lost. We will then be able to follow the proper course of reconciliation with the mother country. That course will not be an easy one, now that blood has been shed on both sides; and who can blame the British for distrusting us after we have so long allowed our vilest members to spew their venom? But take heart. Like a parent who has had to reprimand a disobedient child but still loves that child, the king and Parliament will show us mercy. "From our past experience of the clemency of the King," say the Quakers,

> we have grounds to hope and believe that decent and respectful addresses from those who are vested with legal authority, representing the prevailing dissatisfactions . . . would avail toward obtaining relief, ascertaining and establishing the just rights of the people and restoring the public tranquillity; and we deeply lament that contrary modes of proceeding have been pursued, which have involved the colonies in confusion . . . violence and bloodshed.[5]

1. Samuel Seabury, *Letters of a Westchester Farmer*, in Henry S. Commager and Richard B. Morris, eds., *The Spirit of 'Seventy-Six: The Story of the American Revolution as Told by Participants*, vol. 1. New York: Bobbs-Merrill, 1958, p. 329.

2. Joel Stone, *Narrative*, in Catherine S. Crary, ed., *The Price of Loyalty: Tory Writings from the Revolutionary Era*. New York: McGraw-Hill, 1973, p. 163. Stone actually composed

this piece in 1784, as part of his presentation to the British commission on loyalist claims to property lost in the war. His recollections on this occasion harken back to the tense period of 1775–1776, when, because of his loyalist feelings, he lost his livelihood and also permanently and bitterly parted company with his brother, who was an avowed patriot.

3.   Philadelphia Quakers, *The Ancient Testimony and Principles of the People Called Quakers, Renewed with Respect to the King and Government; and Touching the Commotions Now Prevailing in These and Other Parts of America*, in William Dudley, ed., *The American Revolution*. San Diego: Greenhaven Press, 1992, p. 165.

4.   Jacob Duché, "Letter to George Washington, October 8, 1777," in Crary, *The Price of Loyalty*, pp. 156, 158.

5.   Philadelphia Quakers, *The Ancient Testimony and Principles of the People Called Quakers*, in Dudley, *The American Revolution*, p. 164.

"Our cause is just. Our union is perfect. Our internal resources are great, and, if necessary, foreign assistance is undoubtedly attainable."

A War Against Britain Is More than Justified

A number of Americans are presently of the opinion that this war with Britain can somehow be avoided and that the colonies can find some way to reconcile with the mother country. But they are deluding themselves. From the very beginning, as early as the furor over the Stamp Act in 1765, and probably even earlier, the fateful path toward this war has been the only course available to the colonies. Perhaps the great distance separating us from the parent nation preordained that the two parties would steadily grow apart and undergo a breakdown in understanding and divergence of goals. To this must be added the determined reluctance of a world empire to part with one of the most resourceful and prosperous parts of that empire. The vagaries of geography, time, and national stubbornness, then, seem to have combined to make such a parting a bloody one. John Adams, perhaps our greatest patriot, put it this way:

> A bloody conflict we are destined to endure. This has been my opinion from the beginning. You will

certainly remember my declared opinion was, at the first Congress, when we found that we could not agree upon an immediate non-importation [boycott of British goods], that the contest would not be settled without bloodshed; and that if the hostilities should once commence, they would terminate in an incurable animosity between the two countries. Every political event since the nineteenth of April, 1775 [date of the battles of Lexington and Concord], has confirmed me in this opinion. If you imagine that I flatter myself with [expectations of] happiness and halcyon days after a separation from Great Britain, you are mistaken. . . . I do not expect that our new government will be so quiet as I could wish, nor that happy harmony, confidence and affection between the colonies [will return] for a long time. But freedom is a counterbalance for poverty, discord and war and more. It is your hard lot and mine to be called into life at such a time.[1]

Mr. Adams and his colleagues in the Continental Congress, as well as the colonial legislatures before them, certainly did all they could to avoid this conflict. First, they sent polite petitions; then sterner and more resolute ones; then they refused to buy British goods; then they made peaceful demonstrations; then they dumped tea into the harbor to dramatize their grievances. Meanwhile, the colonists suffered the presence of armed troops in their houses and streets; and finally, these troops moved against them in a naked aggression. It can readily be seen, therefore, that in no way did we provoke the conflict. "Had we begun this quarrel," declared a Philadelphia farmer soon after joining the Continental army,

had we demanded some new privileges unknown to the [British] Constitution, or some commercial licenses incompatible with the general interests of the empire, had we presumed to legislate for Great Britain, or plotted [to overthrow the monarchy], there would then be some plausible apology for the severest hostile treatment we have received. But what have we done? . . . We asserted our rights and petitioned for justice. Was this a crime? . . . We repeated our petitions for redress; was this a crime? We suffered ourselves to be insulted by the introduction of an armed force to dragoon us into obedience;

John Adams, member of the Continental Congress, urged colonists to support separation from Britain.

> we suffered them to take possession of our towns and fortifications, still waiting with decent and anxious expectation [for] justice, humanity, and generosity [from Britain]: was this a crime? . . . Nor did we once lift the sword even in our defense, until provoked to it by a wanton commencement of hostilities on their part.[2]

Yet in spite of our forbearance and peaceful intentions, the British continued, month after month, year after year, to heap injustices on us. There was not only the detestable Stamp Act, but also the long list of wrongs that followed it. "Remember the broken promise of the [British] ministry, never again to attempt a tax on America," an anonymous Philadelphian recently stated. "Remember the duty [Townshend] act. Remember the massacre at Boston, by British soldiers."[3] We should remember too the harsh punishment of Boston for the mere loss of some foreign tea; the shrieks and cries of the wives and children of the men who fell dead on Lexington green under a hail of British musketballs; and the subsequent attacks by bloodthirsty redcoats on Americans in a number of colonial towns.

There can be little doubt, therefore, that Britain means to prosecute a war against us until we bend to its will. As the Continental Congress stated in July 1775, "We are reduced to the alternative of choosing an unconditional submission to the tyranny of irritated ministers or resistance by force. The latter is our choice." We have weighed the costs of a war with the mother country and find it preferable to condemning ourselves and our descendants to voluntary slavery. And so, though we do not want war,

> our cause is just. Our union is perfect. Our internal resources are great, and, if necessary, foreign assistance is undoubtedly attainable. . . . We most solemnly, before God and the world, *declare*, that exerting the utmost energy of those powers which our beneficent Creator hath graciously bestowed

The bloodshed of innocent men at the Battle of Lexington prompted many colonists to join the fight for independence.

upon us, the arms we have been compelled by our enemies to assume, we will, in defiance of every hazard, with unabating firmness and perseverance, employ [work] for the preservation of our liberties; being with one mind resolved to die freemen, rather then to live slaves.[4]

Perhaps America will suffer great privations in this war; but it is certain that she will also learn great lessons, both about herself and her place in the world. It is to be hoped that on the anvil of battle and death we will forge something noble and lasting. Once more, Mr. Adams tells it best:

It is the will of Heaven that the two countries should be sundered forever. It may be the will of Heaven that America shall suffer calamities still more wasting, and distress yet more dreadful. If this is to be the case, it will have this good effect at least. It will inspire us with many virtues which we have not, and correct many errors, follies and vices which threaten to disturb, dishonor and destroy us. The furnace of affliction produces refinement, in states as well as individuals. And the new governments we are assuming in every part will require a purification from our vices, and an augmentation of our virtues, or they will be no blessings.[5]

1. John Adams, "Letter to Samuel Chase, July 1, 1776," in Henry S. Commager and Richard B. Morris, eds., *The Spirit of 'Seventy-Six: The Story of the American Revolution as Told by Participants*, vol. 1. New York: Bobbs-Merrill, 1958, pp. 308–309.

2. "Speech by a Farmer of Philadelphia on Joining the Continental Army, May 1776," in Alden T. Vaughan, ed., *Chronicles of the Revolution*. New York: Grosset and Dunlap, 1965, p. 235.

3. "Memento to Americans, March 1776," in Vaughan, *Chronicles*, p. 228.

4. "Declaration of Causes of Taking Up Arms, July 6, 1775," in Samuel Eliot Morison, ed., *Sources and Documents Illustrating the American Revolution, 1764–1788, and the Formation of the Federal Constitution*. Oxford: Clarendon Press, 1953, pp. 144–45.

5. John Adams, "Letter to Abigail Adams, July 3, 1776," in Commager and Morris, *The Spirit of 'Seventy-Six*, vol. 1, p. 321.

"What sense is there in facing off with the most powerful nation in the world? Any military expert will tell you it is a foolhardy endeavor."

The Americans Have No Chance of Winning

Going to war with Great Britain is utter folly. Consider that, so far, the colonists have been able to petition, lecture, insult, and make demands on the mother country with relative impunity. Consider also that the British presently have relatively few troops stationed on American soil, only a small portion of their total strength in warships patrol American waters, and they have prudently refrained from large-scale military retribution (the incidents at Concord and Lexington were minor skirmishes provoked by the colonists). These factors have apparently imparted a spirit of overconfidence to the rebels, who grow increasingly bold in their protests and verbal attacks with each passing day.

But now consider that this arrogant and dangerous path can lead only to disaster, not only for the rebels, who bear the responsibility of inflaming this conflict, but for all the many innocent residents of the colonies who want nothing else but peace and happiness under British rule. "Do you think . . . that Great Britain is like an old, wrinkled, withered, worn-out hag, whom every jackanapes [impudent rascal] . . . may insult with impunity?" Reverend Samuel Seabury asks the rebels in his pamphlet calling for reconciliation with Britain:

> You will find her a vigorous matron, just approaching a green old age; and with spirit and strength sufficient to chastise her undutiful and rebellious children. Your [insulting and rebellious] measures have as yet produced none of the effects you looked for: Great Britain is not as yet intimidated; she has already a considerable fleet and army in America; more ships and troops are expected in the spring; every appearance indicates a design in her to support her claim [over the colonies] with vigor.[1]

Indeed, far from being intimidated, Britain will fight; and, as she did in the still memorable war against the French and Indians, she will send across the Atlantic whatever forces she feels are necessary to achieve victory. What sense is there in facing off with the most powerful nation in the world? Any military expert will tell you it is a foolhardy endeavor. Consider the words of the great general Thomas Gage himself, who has had the poor luck of being saddled with the task of dealing with these irate rebels. "What fools you are," he told them in 1775,

> to pretend to resist the power of Great Britain; she maintained [in the] last war [the French and Indian War] three hundred thousand men, and will do the same now rather than suffer the ungrateful people of this country to continue in their rebellion.[2]

Another illustrious British officer, Major John Pitcairn, agrees that the mother country's military prowess gives it the overwhelming advantage. "I am satisfied," he has said, "that one active campaign, a smart action, and burning two or three of their towns, will set everything to rights. Nothing now, I am afraid, but this will ever convince those foolish bad people that England is in earnest."[3]

It might be argued that because these officers are British, their opinions must be biased and therefore off the mark. Yet their assessments of the situation are well supported by noted colonials, among them the honorable Charles Inglis of New York. In a popular pamphlet published in Philadelphia in 1776, he states:

> Devastation and ruin must mark the progress of this war along the seacoast of America. Hitherto, Britain has not exerted her power. Her number of troops and ships of war here at present is very little more than she judged expedient in time of peace—the former does not amount to 12,000 men—nor the latter

The Battle of Lexington propelled American colonists to wage war against Britain.

to 40 ships, including frigates. . . . The seas have been open to our ships; and, although some skirmishes have unfortunately happened, yet a ray of hope still cheered both sides that peace was not distant. But, as soon as we declare for independence, every prospect of this kind must vanish. Ruthless war, with all its aggravated horrors, will ravage our once happy land; our seacoasts and ports will be ruined, and our ships taken. Torrents of blood will be spilled, and thousands reduced to beggary and wretchedness.[4]

Addressing the situation from another vantage, while the British possess vast military and other resources, the colonies clearly do not. "What have the Americans to oppose such mighty power?" the *Virginia Gazette* recently inquired. The *Gazette*'s answer: America has no navy to defend its long coastline; no large-scale manufacturing base, as Britain does, to provide the masses of supplies necessary to wage a war; no national treasury and very little money with which to establish one; and "an army without clothing, arms, ammunition or discipline."[5] Indeed, this sore lack of military provisions has prompted Jacob Duché, rector of Christ Church in Philadelphia, to write to General George Washington, imploring him to see reason and give up the fight:

Where are your resources? O my dear sir! How sadly have you been abused by a faction [the rebel leaders] void of truth and void of tenderness to you and your country? . . . The spirit of the whole nation [of England] is in full activity against you. . . . All orders and ranks of men in Great Britain are now unanimous and determined to risk their all in the contest. . . . In a word, your harbors are blocked up, your cities [will] fall one after another, fortress after fortress, battle after battle, [will be] lost.[6]

As if such portents of doom are not enough to scare America into thinking straight, there is still another; namely, without Britain's protection, who will defend the frontiers against the Indian menace? A Georgia newspaper has rightly addressed this fearful problem, one that all the colonies face: "In a word . . . there is a great danger of an Indian war . . . and that [in] the event of it, should we, by our conduct, forfeit the protection of our mother country . . . inevitable ruin to this province is certain."[7]

Even if, by some miracle, the colonies were able to win such a war against so great a power, the end result would still be ruin for America. On the one hand, as Mr. Inglis warns, Britain, enraged by her loss, would probably "parcel out this continent to the different European powers." Spain would get Florida back, France would reacquire Canada, and other Europeans "might come in for a portion."[8] In short, we would then find ourselves having to fight all of Europe, an enterprise that would utterly consume and destroy us. Equally possible is our being consumed by a calamitous *civil* war. "Even a final victory would effectively ruin us," states New Jersey's Thomas Chandler, "as it would necessarily introduce civil wars among us. . . . And till one part of this country shall have subdued the other . . . this peaceful region must become . . . a theater of inconceivable misery and horror."[9]

In light of these ominous and destructive probabilities, we should break off hostilities immediately and sue for peace terms. Our very lives, fortunes, and futures depend on this rational and prudent course of action.

1. Samuel Seabury, *Letters of a Westchester Farmer*, in Henry S. Commager and Richard B. Morris, eds., *The Spirit of 'Seventy-Six: The Story of the American Revolution as Told by Participants*, vol. 1. New York: Bobbs-Merrill, 1958, p. 329.

2. Quoted by Major John Pitcairn, in "Letter to the Earl of Sandwich, March 4, 1775," in Commager and Morris, *The Spirit of 'Seventy-Six*, vol. 1, p. 62.

3. Pitcairn, "Letter to the Earl of Sandwich," in Commager and Morris, *The Spirit of 'Seventy-Six*, vol. 1, p. 62.

4. Charles Inglis, *The True Interest of America Impartially Stated, in Certain Strictures on a Pamphlet Intitled Common Sense*, in William Dudley, ed., *The American Revolution*. San Diego: Greenhaven Press, 1992, pp. 154–55.

5. *Virginia Gazette*, February 3, 1776, quoted in Philip Davidson, *Propaganda and the American Revolution, 1763–1783*. New York: W.W. Norton, 1973, p. 289.

6. Jacob Duché, "Letter to George Washington, October 8, 1777," in Catherine S. Crary, ed., *The Price of Loyalty: Tory Writings from the Revolutionary Era*. New York: McGraw-Hill, 1973, p. 157.

7. *Georgia Gazette*, August 10, 1774, quoted in Davidson, *Propaganda*, p. 289 n. 76.

8. Inglis, *The True Interest of America*, in Dudley, *The American Revolution*, p. 155.

9. Thomas Chandler, *What Think Ye of the Congress Now?* quoted in Davidson, *Propaganda*, p. 289.

"Our cruel and unrelenting foe leaves us no choice but a brave resistance, or the most abject submission. . . . Let us therefore . . . show the world that free men contending for liberty on their own ground are superior to any slavish mercenary on earth."

The Americans Can and Will Win the War

Despite nay-saying loyalist rhetoric and some worries even among the ranks of patriots, Americans have every reason to be optimistic about their chances of winning this war against Great Britain. No one can deny that the enemy possesses the most formidable military establishment in the world. Yet wars are not always won simply on the basis of which side has the most troops, ships, and guns. The specific physical and logistical circumstances of a conflict, along with psychological and other factors, must be considered as well.

For instance, though strong and organized, Britain faces certain logistical obstacles that will make its prosecution of this war exceedingly difficult. First, the British are still in debt from the last war (the Seven Years' War, or French and Indian War), as they have consistently reminded us of late in defending their policies of taxing the colonies. Spain and France, her enemies in that war, are not likely to lend Britain money, nor will very many other Europeans, who would be very happy to see Britain's fortunes falter. Second, with the American colonies in

A group of armed patriots, called minutemen, pledged to join the fight against the British at a minute's notice.

revolt, a large and valuable portion of Britain's trade and revenue, on which it has come to depend, has been cut off.

Now add to these factors another even more telling, namely the tremendous distance separating the colonies from the mother country. One of our leading patriots, New Jersey's William Livingston, points out: "We ought to consider the amazing expense and difficulty of transporting troops and provisions above three thousand miles, with the impossibility of recruiting their army at a less distance."[1] We need not take only the word of an American on this point. In 1775, Edmund Burke, one of Britain's most distinguished legislators, stood before Parliament's House of Commons and delivered this stirring caution:

> Three thousand miles of ocean lie between you and them. No contrivance can prevent the effect of this distance, in weakening government. Seas roll, and

months pass, between the order and the execution: and the want of a speedy explanation of a single point is enough to defeat a whole system. You have, indeed, winged ministers of vengeance [warships], who carry their bolts [weapons] in their pounces [claws] to the remotest verge of the sea. But there a [higher, natural or divine] power steps in, that limits the arrogance of raging passions and furious elements, and says, "So far shalt thou go, and no farther."[2]

Moreover, a good many residents of Britain—leaders, workers, and soldiers alike—lack the will and enthusiasm needed to win so great a conflict fought over such great distances. Once again, recognition of British weakness comes straight from the horse's mouth, so to speak; Mr. Johnstone, member of Parliament and former governor of Florida, recently told the House of Commons that the hearts of Englishmen are not in a fight with their fellow Englishmen in the colonies:

> I maintain that the sense of the best and wisest men in this country are on the side of the Americans; that three to one in Ireland are on their side; that the soldiers and sailors feel an unwillingness to the service; that you never will find the same exertions of spirit in this as in other wars. I speak it to the credit of the fleet and army: they do not like to butcher men whom the greatest characters in this country consider as contending in the glorious cause of preserving those institutions which are necessary to the happiness, security and elevation of the human mind.[3]

The day after Mr. Johnstone's speech, his colleague, Mr. Adair, pointed out another drawback of the war with America that could only further lower British morale. Even if the British achieved victory, he declared, they would in fact be abject losers, for if

> a full exertion of all the powers and resources of this kingdom, which I am far from thinking the most

probable event, should at length, after a long and obstinate contest . . . prevail over every effort of liberty, reduce the colonies to a forced submission, and complete the conquest of America—in what respect shall we be gainers by such a conquest? What shall we acquire at such an expense but the empty assertion of an unprofitable sovereignty over desolated provinces, or a few miserable slaves? Instead of those flourishing dominions, the wealth and commerce of which has rendered us the greatest nation in the world, we shall find ourselves possessed of a vast territory, which, drained of the sources from whence that greatness flowed . . . will not only be useless and unprofitable, but burdensome and destructive.[4]

To these British disadvantages in the impending conflict we can add certain American advantages. First, we are fighting on our own ground, in defense of our homes, families, and way of life; and just as the tiny Greek city-states fought with unprecedented valor and in the end defeated the mighty Persian colossus in one of the great wars of history, so shall we prevail.[5] What is more, we are also fighting for liberty, while the enemy soldiers fight because they are ordered or, in the case of their mercenaries, paid to do so. On July 4, 1776, a young private in the rebel army encamped in New York wrote home to his parents:

The time is now near at hand which must probably determine whether Americans are to be free men or slaves. . . . The fate of unborn millions will now depend . . . on the courage and conduct of this army. Our cruel and unrelenting foe leaves us no choice but a brave resistance, or the most abject submission. . . . Let us therefore . . . show the world that free men contending for liberty on their own ground are superior to any slavish mercenary on earth.[6]

Finally, consider that God is with us. Surely he recognizes the righteousness of our cause and purity of our intentions, and conversely, the unwholesome intentions of our opponents. As our great patriotic writer Tom Paine has put it:

> God Almighty will not give up a people to military destruction . . . who have so earnestly . . . sought to avoid the calamities of war by every decent method which wisdom could invent. . . . I cannot see on what grounds the king of Britain can look up to Heaven for help against us: a common murderer, a highwayman or a house-breaker has as good a pretense [to seek God's help] as he.[7]

1. William Livingston, "Speech to New Jersey Legislature, February 25, 1777," in Alden T. Vaughan, ed., *Chronicles of the Revolution*. New York: Grosset and Dunlap, 1965, p. 249.

2. Edmund Burke, "Speech to British House of Commons, March 22, 1775," in Max Beloff, ed., *The Debate on the American Revolution, 1761–1783*. London: Adam and Charles Black, 1960, p. 211.

3. Mr. Johnstone, "Speech to British House of Commons, October 26, 1775," in Henry S. Commager and Richard B. Morris, eds., *The Spirit of 'Seventy-Six: The Story of the American Revolution as Told by Participants*, vol. 1. New York: Bobbs-Merrill, 1958, p. 260.

4. Serjeant Adair, "Speech to British House of Commons, October 27, 1775," in Commager and Morris, *The Spirit of 'Seventy-Six*, vol. 1, p. 263.

5. The better-educated American patriots often referred to famous ancient conflicts and compared themselves to Greek and Roman patriots. Here, the reference is to the Greek and Persian Wars, in which, in 480 B.C., the Persian Empire, then the greatest on earth, invaded Greece with forces estimated at over two hundred thousand troops and one thousand ships. Thirty-one Greek city-states formed a defensive coalition and, against seemingly impossible odds, defeated the invaders repeatedly both on sea and land. This David-and-Goliath victory saved Europe from Asian domination and paved the way for Greece's cultural golden age and the ultimate triumph of Western civilization.

6. Quoted in Philip Davidson, *Propaganda and the American Revolution, 1763–1783*. New York: W.W. Norton, 1973, p. 341.

7. Thomas Paine, *The Crisis*, in William Dudley, ed., *The American Revolution*. San Diego: Greenhaven Press, 1992, p. 182.

CHAPTER 4

Modern Historians Debate the Meaning of the Revolution

"The stream of revolution, once started, could not be confined within narrow banks, but spread abroad upon the land. Many economic desires, many social aspirations were set free by the political struggle, many aspects of colonial society profoundly altered by the forces thus let loose."

The War of Independence Was a Social Revolution

One of the most controversial questions about America's past that twentieth-century historians have asked and tentatively answered is whether the American Revolution was a social revolution. Some say it was merely a political revolution in which Americans traded domination by foreign aristocrats for a similar brand of rule by members of the American social elite, leaving society itself more or less unchanged. Others hold that the struggle for independence brought about profound changes at many levels of American society, making it a social as well as a political revolution.

Most scholars concede that the making of a social revolution requires radical leaders with radical views. Were the Revolution's leaders radicals? Obviously, John Adams, Thomas Jefferson, George Washington, and other leading patriots were not part of an oppressed class. As noted scholar Gordon S. Wood points out, "They had no crushing imperial chains to throw off. In fact, the colonists knew that they were freer, more equal, more prosperous, and less burdened with cumbersome feudal and monarchical restraints than any other part of mankind in the eighteenth century."[1] So, unlike the revolutionaries of the French, Russian, and other major world revolutions, the American patriots were not advocating and fighting for radical changes in society.

The framers of the Declaration of Independence set the stage for freedom.

What made the American revolutionaries radical for their time was their advocacy of a then very unorthodox political and social idea—independence. In fact, the differences of opinion that had divided the American colonists before and during the Revolutionary War had revolved mainly around the issue of dependence versus independence. All Americans cherished personal freedom and other long-standing rights enjoyed by Englishmen; therefore, despite the rhetoric of the Declaration of Independence and other revolutionary documents and speeches, the conflict was not about the lack of personal freedom. Instead, the core difference between loyalists and patriots was that the loyalists wished to continue exercising their personal freedoms under the umbrella of British rule; while the revolutionaries desired to do so on their own, as a separate people with their own unique national identity. Before the Revolution, the idea that society should consist of various classes, each dependent on the one above it, with the highest class, the nobility, itself dependent on a king, was the accepted norm both in Europe and America. The American revolutionaries rejected this idea and began equating dependency with slavery. "There are but two sorts of men in the world," stated John Adams in 1775, "free men and slaves."[2] The American Revolution, then, was an attack on the idea of political and social dependency and as such was highly radical for its time.

Regardless of the patriots' championing of a radical idea, some scholars argue, at the close of the Revolutionary War the only major changes wrought by the conflict were political in nature. In this scenario, American leaders proceeded to reorganize and reshape government; but society itself remained more or less the same, retaining the same old class divisions, second-class citizenship of women, and cruel enslavement of blacks. But this is a shortsighted evaluation that assumes that the Revolution was over in 1783. In reality, it had only just begun. Initially, it is true, the members of the traditional all-white male elite were the principal beneficiaries of the new order; however, these men set up a government that firmly established the ideals of equality and a democratic society; and although these concepts existed mainly on paper at first, over time increasing numbers of Americans of all walks of life came to see them as their birthright and demand to benefit from them. In his classic statement of social revolution, historian J. Franklin Jameson writes:

> The stream of revolution, once started, could not be confined within narrow banks, but spread abroad upon the land. Many economic desires, many social aspirations were set free by the political struggle, many aspects of colonial society profoundly altered by the forces thus let loose. The relations of social classes to one another, the institution of slavery, the system of land-holding, the course of business, the forms and spirit of the intellectual and religious life, all felt the transforming hand of revolution, all emerged from under it in shapes advanced many degrees nearer to those we know.[3]

Indeed, the Revolution's "transforming hand," still deeply rooted in its hatred and rejection of dependency, set in motion the ideological and social forces that reshaped American society. In each succeeding generation, group after group became in a sense new revolutionaries who took Adams, Jefferson, and the others at their word, demanded their rights, and finally, often after long and difficult struggles, shook off their own dependencies. Antislavery societies first formed in America during the revolutionary period. Their increasing strength, combined with other changing social and economic factors, led inevitably to the Civil War and the abolition of slavery. Women likewise lobbied for and gained civil rights, including the right to vote. Meanwhile, nearly all of the class and economic barriers that had existed in the late 1700s were swept away in the continuing American Revolution. "In 1760," Wood remarks,

America was only a collection of disparate colonies huddled along a narrow strip of the Atlantic coast— economically underdeveloped outposts existing on the very edges of the civilized world. The less than two million monarchical subjects who lived in these colonies still took for granted that society was and ought to be a hierarchy [ladder] of ranks and degrees of dependency and that most people were bound together by personal ties of one sort or another. Yet scarcely fifty years later these insignificant border- land provinces had become a giant, almost continent- wide republic of nearly ten million egalitarian-minded bustling citizens who not only had thrust them- selves into the vanguard [forefront] of history, but had fundamentally altered their society and their social relationships. Far from remaining monarchical, hierarchy-ridden subjects on the margin of civiliza- tion, Americans had become, almost overnight, the most liberal, the most democratic, the most commer- cially minded, and the most modern people in the world.[4]

These sweeping social changes continued and in fact accel- erated in the twentieth century, as seen in battle after battle by one minority group after another for civil rights, justice, and fair treatment under the majestic constitutional framework created by the Founding Fathers. Thus, in breaking away from Britain and constructing the Constitution, a mighty blueprint for human freedom from dependency, the American revolutionaries set in motion a social revolution that contin- ues to the present. That framework, that blueprint, and that continuing revolution are what make America great.

1. Gordon S. Wood, *The Radicalism of the American Revolution*. New York: Knopf, 1992, p. 4.

2. Quoted in William Dudley, ed., *The American Revolution*. San Diego: Greenhaven Press, 1992, p. 265.

3. J. Franklin Jameson, *The American Revolution Considered as a Social Movement*. Princeton, NJ: Princeton University Press, 1926, p. 9.

4. Wood, *The Radicalism of the American Revolution*, p. 8.

*"The reality behind the Declaration of Independence . . .
was that a rising class of important people needed to enlist
on their side enough Americans to defeat England, without
disturbing too much the relations of wealth and power that
had developed over 150 years of colonial history."*

The War of Independence Was Not a Social Revolution

The American War of Independence was not a social revolution because the leading revolutionaries were not radicals seeking to overthrow the old order and establish a new society. They were instead conservative gentlemen attempting to maintain the status quo. For a long time the American colonies had enjoyed a great deal of autonomy, free from major British military and economic intervention; and well-to-do landholding Americans, the New World equivalent of the older British gentry, had come to control the local colonial legislatures. When, in the 1760s, the mother country began to assert more overt economic and military controls over the colonists, the American elite decided that the only way to perpetuate their comfortable way of life was to break away from Britain. "The Americans of 1776," writes noted historian Clinton Rossiter, were among the first men in modern history to defend rather than seek an open society and constitutional liberty; their political faith, like the appeal to arms it supported, was therefore surprisingly sober. . . . By 1765, the colonies had achieved a society more open, an economy more fluid, and a government more constitutional than anything Europeans would know for years to come. Americans had secured and were ready to defend a condition of freedom that other liberty-minded men could only hope for in the distant future or plot for in the brutal present. The political theory of the American Revolution, in contrast to that of the French Revolution, was not a theory designed to make the world over. The world—at least the American corner of it—had already been made over as thoroughly as any sensible man could imagine. . . . [The revolutionaries'] goal therefore was simply to consolidate, then expand by cautious stages, the large measure of liberty and property that was part of their established way of life.[1]

To accomplish their goal—the establishment of a new nation ruled by the same old colonial elite—the revolution's leaders needed the support of the lower classes; and through revolutionary rhetoric and propaganda they skillfully persuaded many common Americans to support the cause of independence. This, historian Howard Zinn contends, was the beginning of "the mobilization of lower-class energy by upper-class politicians, for their own purposes,"[2] a kind of manipulation that has continued throughout American history to the present.

It is important to realize that in mobilizing the lower classes to fight the British the revolutionary leaders did not envision overhauling society in order to give lower-class Americans a political voice equal to their own. The members of the elite thought it perfectly natural that society should be

guided by men like themselves; they, like their British coun-
terparts, feared the common masses, the "mob," the "great
beast" that was, they believed, by itself incapable of intelli-
gent, ordered rule; and it was therefore imperative to control
the mob while marshaling its energies. This task, Zinn sug-
gests, was tricky:

> Fortunately for the Revolutionary movement, the
> key battles were being fought in the North, and
> here, in the cities, the colonial leaders had a divided
> white population; they could win over the mechan-
> ics, who were a kind of middle class, who had a stake
> in the fight against England, who faced competition
> from English manufacturers. The biggest problem
> was to keep the propertyless people, who were un-
> employed and hungry . . . under control. In Boston,
> the economic grievances of the lowest classes min-
> gled with anger against the British and exploded
> in mob violence. The leaders of the Independence
> movement wanted to use that mob energy against
> England, but also to contain it so that it would not
> demand too much from them.[3]

The members of the lower economic classes were not the
only people exploited, left out, or marginalized by the Revolution. Neither women, black slaves, white servants, nor
minors benefited directly from the ideals of the Declaration
of Independence, since the ruling elite, the "men" of the
phrase "all men are created equal," considered it only natural
that they should control these groups, too. As George Washington University scholar Linda G. DePauw states, together
these groups

> comprised approximately 80 percent of the two and a
> half million Americans in the year 1776. The legal
> doctrine applied to these classes excluded them from
> the category of persons who should enjoy the "inalien-
> able rights" of which the Declaration speaks. But per-
> haps the most significant part of their unfreedom was

their usual lack of a right to vote. . . . Indeed, the very word "enfranchise" [empower with voting rights] was defined in the eighteenth century as the equivalent of the word "emancipate"; it meant "to make free."[4]

According to some historians, the Declaration of Independence was a tool used by revolutionary leaders to rally the support of the lower classes against Britain.

THE DECLARATION OF INDEPENDENCE   as printed by order of Congress by John Dunlap of Phila-

None of these groups gained either the franchise or emancipation during or immediately following the Revolution; and their social status, as well as most other important aspects of society, remained unchanged.

Therefore, the American achievement of independence was a political rather than social revolution in which the members of the local ruling elite were able to maintain their power and position while eliminating foreign competition and intervention. Zinn effectively sums up how the old guard managed to perpetuate the inequalities of the traditional status quo:

> The reality behind the Declaration of Independence . . . was that a rising class of important people needed to enlist on their side enough Americans to defeat England, without disturbing too much the relations of wealth and power that had developed over 150 years of colonial history. . . . The Declaration . . . was read, with all its flaming radical language, from the town hall balcony in Boston. . . . Four days after the reading, the Boston Committee of Correspondence ordered the townsmen to show up on the Common for a military draft. The rich, it turned out, could avoid the draft by paying for substitutes; the poor had to serve. This led to rioting, and shouting: "Tyranny is tyranny, let it come from whom it may."[5]

1. Clinton Rossiter, *Seedtime of the Republic: The Origin of the American Tradition of Political Liberty*. New York: Harcourt, Brace and World, 1953, pp. 440, 448.

2. Howard Zinn, *A People's History of the United States*. New York: HarperCollins, 1980, pp. 60–61.

3. Zinn, *People's History*, p. 65.

4. Quoted in William Dudley, ed., *The American Revolution*. San Diego: Greenhaven Press, 1992, p. 248.

5. Zinn, *People's History*, pp. 74–75.

APPENDIX

Excerpts from Original Documents Pertaining to the American Revolution

Document 1: Taxation of the Colonies Defended

In a 1765 pamphlet titled The Objections to the Taxation of Our American Colonies by the Legislature of Great Britain, Briefly Considered, *Soame Jenyns, a member of Parliament and the British Board of Trade, argued that, despite American claims, all Englishmen were taxed without their consent, and also that the colonists were represented in Parliament in the "virtual" sense.*

The right of the Legislature of Great Britain to impose taxes on her American colonies, and the expediency of exerting that right in the present conjuncture, are propositions so indisputably clear that I should never have thought it necessary to have undertaken their defence, had not many arguments been lately flung out both in papers and conversation, which with insolence equal to their absurdity deny them both. As these are usually mixt up with several patriotic and favorite words such as liberty, property, Englishmen, etc., which are apt to make strong impressions on that more numerous part of mankind who have ears but no understanding, it will not, I think, be improper to give them some answers. To this, therefore, I shall singly confine myself, and do it in as few words as possible, being sensible that the fewest will give least trouble to myself, and probably most information to my reader.

The great capital argument which I find on this subject, and which, like an elephant at the head of a Nabob's [Indian ruler's] army, being once overthrown must put the whole into confusion, is this; that no Englishman is, or can be taxed, but by his own consent: by which must be meant one of these three propositions; either that no Englishman can be taxed without his own consent as an individual; or that no Englishman can be taxed without the consent of the persons he chuses to represent him; or that no Englishman can be taxed without the consent of the majority of all those who are elected by himself and others of his fellow subjects to represent them. Now let us impartially consider whether any one of these propositions are in fact true: if not, then this wonderful structure which has been erected upon them falls at once to the ground, and like another Babel, perishes by a confusion of words, which the builders themselves are unable to understand.

First then, that no Englishman is or can be taxed but by his own consent as an individual: this is so far from being true, that it is the very reverse of truth; for no man that I know of is taxed by his own consent, and an Englishman, I believe, is as little likely to be so taxed as any man in the world.

Secondly, that no Englishman is or can be taxed but by the consent of those persons whom he has chose to represent him. For the truth of this I shall appeal only to the candid representatives of those unfortunate counties which produce cyder, and shall willingly acquiesce under their determination. [Jenyns here refers to an unpopular tax levied on cider in some counties in Britain in 1764.]

Lastly, that no Englishman is or can be taxed without the consent of the majority of those who are elected by himself and others of his fellow subjects to represent them. This is certainly as false as the other two; for every Englishman is taxed, and not one in twenty represented: copyholders, leaseholders, and all men possessed of personal property only, chuse no representatives; Manchester, Birmingham, and many more of our richest and most flourishing trading towns send no members to Parliament, consequently cannot consent by their representatives, because they chuse none to represent them; yet are they not Englishmen? or are they not taxed?

I am well aware that I shall hear Lock, Sidney, Selden, and many other great names quoted to prove that every Englishman, whether he has a right to vote for a representative or not, is still represented in the British Parliament, in which opinion they all agree. On what principle of common-sense this opinion is founded I comprehend not, but on the authority of such respectable names I shall acknowledge its truth; but then I will ask one question, and on that I will rest the whole merits of the cause. Why does not this imaginary representation extend to America as well as over the whole Island of Great Britain? If it can travel three hundred miles, why not three thousand? if it can jump over rivers and mountains, why cannot it sail over the ocean? If the towns of Manchester and Birmingham, sending no representatives to Parliament, are notwithstanding there represented, why are not the cities of Albany and Boston equally represented in that Assembly? Are they not alike British subjects? are they not Englishmen? or are they only Englishmen when they sollicit for protection, but not Englishmen when taxes are required to enable this country to protect them?

Samuel Eliot Morison, ed., *Sources and Documents Illustrating the American Revolution, 1764–1788, and the Formation of the Federal Constitution.* Oxford: Clarendon Press, 1953, pp. 18–20.

Document 2: Virginia Objects to the Stamp Act

On May 30, 1765, the Virginia legislature passed all but the last two of these resolves, introduced by Patrick Henry, protesting the tax levied by the Stamp Act, which Parliament passed on March 22 of that year.

Resolved, That the first adventurers and settlers of this His Majesty's Colony and Dominion of Virginia brought with them, and transmitted to their posterity, and all other of His Majesty's subjects since inhabiting this His Majesty's said Colony, all the liberties, privileges, franchises, and immunities, that have at any time been held, enjoyed, and possessed, by the people of Great Britain.

Resolved, That by two royal charters, granted by King James the First, the colonists aforesaid are declared entitled to all liberties, privileges, and immunities of denizens and natural subjects, to all intents and purposes, as if they had been abiding and born within the realm of England.

Resolved, That the taxation of the people by themselves, or by persons chosen by themselves to represent them, who can only know what taxes the people are able to bear, or the easiest method of raising them, and must themselves be affected by every tax laid on the people, is the only security against a burthensome taxation, and the distinguishing characteristick of British freedom, without which the ancient constitution cannot exist.

Resolved, That His Majesty's liege people of this his most ancient and loyal Colony have without interruption enjoyed the inestimable right of being governed by such laws, respecting their internal polity and taxation, as are derived from their own consent, with the approbation of their sovereign, or his substitute; and that the same hath never been forfeited or yielded up, but hath been constantly recognized by the kings and people of Great Britain.

Resolved therefore, That the General Assembly of this Colony have the only and sole exclusive right and power to lay taxes and impositions upon the inhabitants of this Colony, and that every attempt to vest such power in any person or persons whatsoever other than the General Assembly aforesaid has a manifest tendency to destroy British as well as American freedom.

Resolved, That His Majesty's liege people, the inhabitants of this Colony are not bound to yield obedience to any law or ordinance whatever, designed to impose any taxation whatsoever upon them other than the laws or ordinances of the General Assembly aforesaid.

Resolved, That any person who shall, by speaking or writing, assert or maintain that any person or persons other than the General Assembly of this Colony, have any right or power to impose or lay any taxation on the people here, shall be deemed an enemy to His Majesty's Colony.

Max Beloff, ed., *The Debate on the American Revolution, 1761–1783.* London: Adam and Charles Black, 1960, pp. 70–73.

Document 3: Parliament Questions Ben Franklin

On February 13, 1766, the British Parliament questioned American colonial representative Benjamin Franklin, who explained why Americans so vigorously protested the Stamp Act, including their objection to being taxed without their "common consent."

Q. What is your name, and place of abode?

A. Franklin, of Philadelphia.

Q. Do the Americans pay any considerable taxes among themselves?

A. Certainly many, and very heavy taxes.

Q. What are the present taxes in Pennsylvania, laid by the laws of the colony?

A. There are taxes on all estates real and personal, a poll tax, a tax on all offices, professions, trades and businesses, according to their profits; an excise on all wine, rum, and other spirits; and a duty of £10 per head on all Negroes imported, with some other duties.

Q. For what purposes are those taxes laid?

A. For the support of the civil and military establishments of the country, and to discharge the heavy debt contracted in the last war. . . .

Q. Do you think it right that America should be protected by this country and pay no part of the expense?

A. That is not the case. The Colonies raised, cloathed and payed during the last war, near 25,000 men and spent many millions.

Q. Were you not reimbursed by Parliament?

A. We were only reimbursed what, in your opinion, we had advanced beyond our proportion, or beyond what might reasonably be expected from us; and it was a very small part of what we spent. Pennsylvania, in particular, disbursed about £500,000, and the reimbursements, in the whole, did not exceed £60,000.

Q. You have said that you pay heavy taxes in Pennsylvania. What do they amount to in the pound?

A. The tax on all estates, real and personal is eighteen pence in the pound, fully rated; and the tax on the profits of trade and professions, with other taxes, do, I suppose, make full half a crown in the pound. . . .

Q. Do not you think the people of America would submit to pay the stamp duty if it was moderated?

A. No, never, unless compelled by force of arms. . . .

Q. In what light did the people of America use to consider the Parliament of Great Britain?

A. They considered the Parliament as the great bulwark and security of their liberties and privileges, and always spoke of it with the utmost respect and veneration. Arbitrary ministers, they thought, might possibly, at times, attempt to oppress them; but they relied on it, that the Parliament, on application, would always give redress. They remembered with gratitude, a strong instance of this, when a bill was brought into Parliament with a clause to make royal instructions laws in the colonies, which the House of Commons would not pass, and it was thrown out.

Q. And have they not still the same respect for Parliament?

A. No, it is greatly lessened. . . .

Q. Don't you think they would submit to the Stamp Act, if it was modified, the obnoxious parts taken out, and the duty reduced to some particulars of small moment?

A. No; they will never submit to it.

Q. What is your opinion of a future tax imposed on the same principle with that of the Stamp Act? How would the Americans receive it?

A. Just as they do this. They would not pay it. . . .

Q. Don't you know that there is, in the Pennsylvania charter, an express reservation of Parliament to lay taxes there?

A. I know there is a clause in the charter by which the King grants that he will levy no taxes on the inhabitants, unless it be with the consent of the assembly or by act of Parliament.

Q. How, then, could the assembly of Pennsylvania assert that laying a tax on them by the Stamp Act was an infringement of their rights?

A. They understood it thus; by the same charter, and otherwise, they are entitled to all the privileges and liberties of Englishmen; they find in the great charters, and the petition and declaration of rights, that one of the privileges of English subjects is, that they are not to be taxed but by their common consent. They have therefore relied upon it, from the first settlement of the province, that the Parliament never would, nor could, by color of that clause in the charter, assume a right of taxing them, till it had qualified itself to exercise such right by admitting representatives from the people to be taxed, who ought to make a part of that common consent. . . .

Q. If the Stamp Act should be repealed, would it induce the assemblies of America to acknowledge the rights of Parliament to tax them, and would they erase their resolutions?

A. No, never.

Q. Are there no means of obliging them to erase those resolutions?

A. None that I know of; they will never do it, unless compelled by force of arms.

Q. Is there a power on earth that can force them to erase them?

A. No power, how great soever, can force men to change their opinions. . . .

Q. What used to be the pride of Americans?

A. To indulge in the fashions and manufactures of Great Britain.

Q. What is now their pride?

A. To wear their old clothes over again, till they can make new ones.

Richard B. Morris, ed., *The American Revolution, 1763–1783: A Bicentennial Collection.* Columbia: University of South Carolina Press, 1970, pp. 81–86.

Document 4: A Member of Parliament Supports American Protests

A number of British politicians came out in support of the American cause in the years preceding the Revolutionary War; for example, in his speech of February 24, 1766, to the House of Lords, excerpted here, Sir Charles Pratt (Lord Camden) argued that it was unfair to tax the Americans as long as they had no representatives in Parliament.

My searches have more and more convinced me, that the British parliament have no right to tax the Americans. I shall not therefore consider the Declaratory Bill now lying on your table; for to what purpose, but loss of time, to consider the particulars of a Bill, the very existence of which is illegal, absolutely illegal, contrary to the fundamental laws of nature, contrary to the fundamental laws of this constitution? A constitution grounded on the eternal and immutable laws of nature; a constitution whose foundation and centre is liberty, which sends liberty to every subject, that is or may happen to be within any part of its ample circumference. Nor my lords, is the doctrine new, it is as old as the constitution; it grew up with it; indeed it is its support; taxation and representation are inseparably, united; God hath joined them, no British parliament can separate them; to endeavour to do it, is to stab our very vitals. Nor is this the first time this doctrine has been mentioned; 70 years ago, my lords, a pamphlet was published, recommending the levying a parliamentary tax on one of the colonies; this pamphlet was answered by two others, then much read; these totally deny the power of taxing the colonies; and why? Because the colonies had no representatives in parliament to give consent; no answer, public or private, was given to these pamphlets, no censure passed upon them; men were not startled at the doctrine as either new or illegal, or derogatory to the rights of parliament. I do not mention these pamphlets by way of authority, but to vindicate myself from the imputation of having first broached this doctrine.

My position is this—I repeat it—I will maintain it to my last hour,—taxation and representation are inseparable;—this position is founded on the laws of nature; it is more, it is itself an eternal law of nature; for whatever is a man's own, is absolutely his own; no man hath a right to take it from him without his consent, either expressed by himself or representative; whoever attempts to do it, attempts an injury; whoever does it, commits a robbery; he throws down and destroys the distinction between liberty and slavery. . . .

For these reasons, my lords, I can never give my assent to any bill for taxing the American colonies, while they remain unrepresented; for as to the distinction of virtual representation, it is so absurd as not to deserve an answer; I therefore pass it over with contempt. The forefathers of the Americans did not leave their native country, and subject themselves to every danger and distress, to be reduced to a state of slavery: they did not give up their rights; they looked for protection, and not for chains, from their mother country; by her they expected to be defended in the possession of their property, and not to be deprived of it: for, should the present power continue, there is nothing which they can call their own.

Max Beloff, ed., *The Debate on the American Revolution, 1761–1783*. London: Adam and Charles Black, 1960, pp. 118–24.

Document 5: John Dickinson Attacks the Townshend Acts

John Dickinson originally published his "Letters from a Farmer in Pennsylvania to the Inhabitants of the British Colonies" anonymously in Philadelphia newspapers over the winter of 1767–1768; the letters were reprinted in pamphlet form soon afterward. In these excerpts from Letters 2 and 12, Dickinson warns his readers that the Townshend duties are no less an illegitimate revenue-producing scheme than the Stamp Act had been.

MY DEAR COUNTRYMEN,

There is another late Act of Parliament, which appears to me to be unconstitutional and as destructive to the liberty of these colonies, as that mentioned in my last letter; that is, the Act for granting the duties on paper, glass, etc. [i.e., the Townshend duties].

The Parliament unquestionably possesses a legal authority to regulate the trade of Great Britain and all her colonies. Such an authority is essential to the relation between a mother country and her colonies; and necessary for the common good of all. He, who considers these provinces as States distinct from the British Empire, has very slender notions of justice, or of their interests. We are but parts of a whole; and therefore there must exist a power somewhere to preside, and preserve the connexion in due order. This power is lodged in the Parliament; and we are as much dependent on Great Britain as a perfectly free people can be on another.

I have looked over every statute relating to these colonies, from their first settlement to this time; and I find every one of them founded on this principle till the Stamp Act administration. All before are calculated to regulate trade and preserve or promote a mutually beneficial intercourse between the several constituent parts of the Empire; and though many of them imposed duties on trade, yet those duties were always imposed with design to restrain the commerce of one part, that was injurious to another, and thus to promote the general welfare. The raising a revenue thereby was never intended. Thus the king, by his judges in his courts of justice, imposes fines which all together amount to a very considerable sum and contribute to the support of government: but this is merely a consequence arising from restrictions that only meant to keep peace and prevent confusion; and surely a man would argue very loosely, who should conclude from hence that the king has a right to levy money in general upon his subjects. Never did the British Parliament, till the period above mentioned, think of imposing duties in America *for the purpose of raising a revenue.* . . .

Here we may observe an authority expressly claimed and exerted to impose duties on these colonies; not for the regulation of trade; not for the preservation or promotion of a mutually beneficial intercourse between the several constituent parts of the Empire, heretofore the sole objects of parliamentary institutions; but for the single purpose of levying money upon us.

This I call an innovation; and a most dangerous innovation. It may perhaps be objected that Great Britain has a right to lay what duties she pleases upon her exports, and it makes no difference to us whether they are paid here or there. To this I answer: these colonies require many things for their use, which the laws of Great Britain prohibit them from getting anywhere but from her. Such are paper and glass. That we may legally be bound to pay any general duties on these commodities relative to the regulation of trade, is granted; but we being obliged by the laws to take from Great Britain any special duties imposed on their exportation to us only, with intention to raise a revenue from us only, are as much taxes upon us as those imposed by the Stamp Act.

What is the difference in substance and right whether the same sum is raised upon us by the rates mentioned in the Stamp Act, on the use of paper, or by these duties on the importation of it? It is only the edition of a former book, shifting a sentence from the end to the beginning. . . .

Here then, my dear countrymen, ROUSE yourselves, and behold the ruin hanging over your heads. If you ONCE admit that Great Britain may lay duties upon her exportations to us, *for the purpose of levying money on us only,* she then will have nothing to do but to lay those duties on the articles which she prohibits us to manufacture—and the tragedy of American liberty is finished. . . .

Let these truths be indelibly impressed on our minds—that we cannot be happy without being free—that we cannot be free without being secure in our property—that we cannot be secure in our property if without our consent others may as by right take it away—that taxes imposed on us by Parliament do thus take it away—that duties laid for the sole purpose of raising money are taxes—that attempts to lay such duties should be instantly and firmly opposed—that this opposition can never be effectual unless it is the united effort of these Provinces—that therefore benevolence of temper towards each other and unanimity of councils are essential to the welfare of the whole—and lastly, that for this reason, every man amongst us who in any manner would encourage either dissension, diffidence, or indifference between these colonies is an enemy to himself and to his country.

Samuel Eliot Morison, ed., *Sources and Documents Illustrating the American Revolution, 1764–1788, and the Formation of the Federal Constitution.* Oxford: Clarendon Press, 1953, pp. 38–42, 53.

Document 6: The Loyalists Persecuted

In the early 1770s, increasing numbers of American loyalists became the victims of mob or random violence, including beatings and tarring-and-featherings. These excerpts from a January 31, 1774, letter written by Boston loyalist Ann Hulton describe one such incident and register her fear that America is becoming an uncertain and dangerous place in which to live.

The most shocking cruelty was exercised a few nights ago, upon a poor old man, a tidesman, one Malcolm. He is reckoned creasy, a quarrel was picked with him, he was afterward taken and tarred and feathered. Theres no law that knows a punishment for the greatest crimes beyond what this is of cruel torture. And this instance exceeds any other before it. He was stript stark naked, one of the severest cold nights this winter, his body covered all over with tar, then with feathers, his arm dislocated in tearing off his cloaths. He was dragged in a cart with thousands attending, some beating him with clubs and knocking him out of the cart, then in again. They gave him several severe whippings, at different parts of the town. This spectacle of horror and sportive cruelty was exhibited for about five hours.

The unhappy wretch they say behaved with the greatest intrepidity and fortitude all the while. Before he was taken, [he] defended himself a long time against numbers, and afterwards when under torture they demanded of him to curse his masters, the King, Governor, etc., which they could not make him do, but he still cried, "Curse all traitors!" They brought him to the gallows and put a rope about his neck, saying they would hang him. He said he wished they would, but that they could not, for God was above the Devil. The doctors say that it is impossible this poor creature can live. They say his flesh comes off his back in stakes.

It is the second time he has been tarred and feathered and this is looked upon more to intimidate the judges and others than a spite to the unhappy victim tho' they owe him a grudge for some things particularly. . . .

These few instances amongst many serve to shew the abject state of government and the licentiousness and barbarism of the times. There's no majestrate that dare or will act to suppress the outrages. No person is secure. There are many objects pointed at, at this time, and when once marked out for vengeance, their ruin is certain.

Henry S. Commager and Richard B. Morris, eds., *The Spirit of 'Seventy-Six: The Story of the American Revolution as Told by Participants*. 2 vols. New York: Bobbs-Merrill, 1958, vol. 1, pp. 335–36.

Document 7: American Towns Rally Behind Boston

After the British imposed the Coercive Acts (March–June 1774) and closed Boston's port to punish the city for the Boston Tea Party, hundreds of towns across the colonies rallied behind the beleaguered Bostonians, all expressing their moral support and many sending cartloads of foodstuffs and other supplies. Typical of the supportive letters that poured into Boston was this excerpt from the patriots of Windham, Connecticut.

To the Committee of Correspondence, Boston.

28th June, 1774

Gentlemen,

'Tis with pity, mixed with indignation, that we have beheld the cruel and unmanly attacks made by the British Parliament on the loyal and patriotic Town of Boston, who seem destined to feel the force of ministerial wrath, the whole weight of parliamentary vengeance levelled at them in a manner so replete with cruelty and injustice as must strike every heart with horror, and fill every breast with rage that is not entirely void of every sentiment of honor and justice and callous to all the common feelings of humanity. But when we consider the cause of all these calamities, that it is nothing less, on your part, than a strict adherence to the fundamental principles of the Constitution, which, when attacked, you dared openly to assert and vindicate, and stand foremost in the glorious cause of Liberty, in which you are contending not only for your own, but ours and the common rights of every American; when we reflect that it is this for which you are suffering such horrid cruelties, for which your streets have been stained with blood, and for which you now feel the horrors of a military government, we are overwhelmed with a conflict of tumultuous passions, and filled with that manly ardor which bids us join you hand in hand and suffer with you in the common cause.

Henry S. Commager and Richard B. Morris, eds., *The Spirit of 'Seventy-Six: The Story of the American Revolution as Told by Participants.* 2 vols. New York: Bobbs-Merrill, 1958, vol. 1, p. 31.

Document 8: The Suffolk Resolves

The Suffolk Resolves, drafted by patriot Joseph Warren for a meeting of several towns in the Boston area, were adopted on September 9, 1774, after which Paul Revere rode overland to Philadelphia to deliver them to the Continental Congress, which endorsed them. Among those excerpted here is the ominous eleventh resolve, calling on local colonial militiamen to prepare for potential hostilities.

Whereas the power but not the justice, the vengeance but not the wisdom of Great-Britain, which of old persecuted, scourged, and exiled our fugitive parents from their native shores, now pursues us, their guiltless children, with unrelenting severity: . . . If we arrest the hand which would ransack our pockets, if we disarm the parricide which points the dagger to our bosoms, if we nobly defeat that fatal edict which proclaims a power to frame laws for us in all cases whatsoever, thereby entailing the endless and numberless curses of slavery upon us, our heirs and their heirs forever; if we successfully resist that unparalleled usurpation of unconstitutional power, whereby our capital is robbed of the means of life; whereby the streets of Boston are thronged with military executioners; whereby our coasts are lined and harbours crouded with ships of war; whereby the charter of the colony, that sacred barrier against the encroachments of tyranny, is mutilated and, in effect, annihilated. . . .

Therefore, we have resolved, and do resolve: . . .

3. That the late acts of the British parliament for blocking up the harbour of Boston, for altering the established form of government in this colony, and for screening the most flagitious violators of the laws of the province from a legal trial, are gross infractions of those rights to which we are justly entitled by the laws of nature, the British constitution, and the charter of the province.

4. That no obedience is due from this province to either or any part of the acts above-mentioned, but that they be rejected as the attempts of a wicked administration to enslave America. . . .

7. That it be recommended to the collectors of taxes, constables and all other officers, who have public monies in their hands, to retain the same, and not to make any payment thereof to the provincial county treasurer until the civil government of the province is placed upon a constitutional foundation, or until it shall otherwise be ordered by the proposed provincial Congress. . . .

10. That the late act of parliament for establishing the Roman Catholic religion and the French laws in that extensive country, now called Canada, is dangerous in an extreme degree to the Protestant religion and to the

civil rights and liberties of all America; and, therefore, as men and Protestant Christians we are indispensably obliged to take all proper measures for our security.

11. That whereas our enemies have flattered themselves that they shall make an easy prey of this numerous, brave and hardy people, from an apprehension that they are unacquainted with military discipline; we, therefore, for the honour, defence and security of this county and province, advise, as it has been recommended to take away all commissions from the officers of the militia, that those who now hold commissions, or such other persons, be elected in each town as officers in the militia, as shall be judged of sufficient capacity for that purpose, and who have evidenced themselves the inflexible friends to the rights of the people; and that the inhabitants of those towns and districts, who are qualified, do use their utmost diligence to acquaint themselves with the art of war as soon as possible, and do, for that purpose, appear under arms at least once every week. . . .

14. That until our rights are fully restored to us, we will, to the utmost of our power, and we recommend the same to the other counties, to withhold all commercial intercourse with Great-Britain, Ireland, and the West-Indies, and abstain from the consumption of British merchandise and manufactures, and especially of East-India teas and piece goods, with such additions, alterations, and exceptions only, as the General Congress of the colonies may agree to.

Henry S. Commager and Richard B. Morris, eds., *The Spirit of 'Seventy-Six: The Story of the American Revolution as Told by Participants.* 2 vols. New York: Bobbs-Merrill, 1958, vol. 1, pp. 53–54.

Document 9: Resolves of the First Continental Congress

On October 14, 1774, not long after endorsing the provocative statements of the Suffolk Resolves, the Continental Congress passed its own less radical but firmly resolute resolves, excerpted here.

Whereupon the deputies so appointed being now assembled, in a full and free representation of these colonies, taking into their most serious consideration the best means of attaining the ends aforesaid, do in the first place, as Englishmen their ancestors in like cases have usually done, for asserting and vindicating their rights and liberties, *declare,*

That the inhabitants of the English Colonies in North America, by the immutable laws of nature, the principles of the English Constitution, and the several charters or compacts, have the following rights:

1. That they are entitled to life, liberty, and property, and they have never ceded to any sovereign power whatever, a right to dispose of either without their consent.

2. That our ancestors, who first settled these colonies, were at the time of their emigration from the mother country, entitled to all the rights, liberties, and immunities of free and natural-born subjects within the realm of England.

3. That by such emigration they by no means forfeited, surrendered, or lost any of those rights, but that they were, and their descendants now are entitled to the exercise and enjoyment of all such of them, as their local and other circumstances enable them to exercise and enjoy.

4. That the foundation of English liberty, and of all free government, is a right in the people to participate in their legislative council: and as the English colonists are not represented, and from their local and other circumstances, cannot properly be represented in the British Parliament, they are entitled to a free and exclusive power of legislation in their several provincial legislatures, where their right of representation can alone be preserved, in all cases of taxation and internal polity, subject only to the negative of their sovereign, in such manner as has been heretofore used and accustomed. . . .

7. That these, His Majesty's Colonies, are likewise entitled to all the immunities and privileges granted and confirmed to them by royal charters, or secured by their several codes of provincial laws.

8. That they have a right peaceably to assemble, consider of their grievances, and petition the king; and that all prosecutions, prohibitory proclamations, and commitments for the same, are illegal.

9. That the keeping a standing army in these colonies, in times of peace, without the consent of the legislature of that colony in which such army is kept, is against law. . . .

In the course of our inquiry, we find many infringements and violations of the foregoing rights, which, from an ardent desire that harmony and mutual intercourse of affection and interest may be restored, we pass over for the present, and proceed to state such acts and measures as have been adopted since the last war, which demonstrate a system formed to enslave America. . . . [The document goes on to list the British acts deemed objectionable, including those allowing British troops to be quartered on American soil.]

To these grievous Acts and measures Americans cannot submit, but in hopes that their fellow-subjects in Great Britain will, on a revision of them, restore us to that state in which both countries found happiness and prosperity, we have for the present only resolved to pursue the following peaceable measures: (1) To enter into a non-importation, non-consumption, and non-exportation agreement or association. (2) To prepare an Address to the people of Great Britain, and a Memorial to the inhabitants of British America, and (3) To prepare a loyal Address to His Majesty, agreeable to resolutions already entered into.

Samuel Eliot Morison, ed., *Sources and Documents Illustrating the American Revolution, 1764–1788, and the Formation of the Federal Constitution*. Oxford: Clarendon Press, 1953, pp. 119–22.

Document 10: Britain Not Intimidated

From 1774 on, American loyalist spokesmen typically warned Americans not to defy and provoke Britain into a fight; in this view, because America had no chance against the mother country, reconciliation was the only sensible course. These are the main points made by Reverend Samuel Seabury in this excerpt from his December 1774 pamphlet titled Letters of a Westchester Farmer.

Do you think, Sir, that Great Britain is like an old, wrinkled, withered, worn-out hag, whom every jackanapes that truants along the streets may insult with impunity? You will find her a vigorous matron, just approaching a green old age; and with spirit and strength sufficient to chastise her undutiful and rebellious children. Your measures have as yet produced none of the effects you looked for: Great Britain is not as yet intimidated; she has already a considerable fleet and army in America; more ships and troops are expected in the spring; every appearance indicates a design in her to support her claim with vigour. You may call it *infatuation, madness, frantic extravagance,* to hazard so small a number of troops as she can spare against the thousands of New England. Should the dreadful contest once begin— But God forbid! Save, heavenly Father! O save my country from perdition!

Consider, Sir, is it right to risk the valuable blessings of property, liberty and life, to the single chance of war? Of the worst kind of war—a civil war? a civil war founded on rebellion? Without ever attempting the peaceable mode of accommodation? Without ever asking a redress of our complaints from the only power on earth who can redress them? When disputes happen between nations independent of each other, they first attempt to settle them by their ambassadors; they seldom run hastily to war till they have tried what can be done by treaty and mediation. I would make many more concessions to a parent than were justly due to him, rather than engage with him in a duel. But we are rushing into a war with our parent state without offering the least concession; without even deigning to propose an accommodation. . . . The congress . . . foresaw the horrid tragedy that must be acted in America, should their measures be generally adopted; why else did they advise us "to extend our views to *mournful* events," and be in *all* "respects prepared for *every* contingency?"

May God forgive *them,* but may he confound *their* devices: and may he give *you* repentance and a better mind!

Henry S. Commager and Richard B. Morris, eds., *The Spirit of 'Seventy-Six: The Story of the American Revolution as Told by Participants.* 2 vols. New York: Bobbs-Merrill, 1958, vol. 1, p. 329.

Document 11: America Is Ready to Fight

On July 6, 1775, less than two months after the battles at Lexington and Concord, the Continental Congress issued its Declaration of Causes of Taking Up Arms, *excerpted here. The document was intended to show that American patriots had so far explored all peaceful avenues of settling their differences with the mother country and that, although they did not want to fight, they would do so if necessary.*

A Congress of delegates from the United Colonies was assembled at Philadelphia on the fifth day of last September. We resolved again to offer an humble and dutiful petition to the king, and also addressed our fellow-

subjects of Great Britain. We have pursued every temperate, every respect-
ful measure: we have even proceeded to break off our commercial intercourse with our fellow-subjects, as the last peaceable admonition that our
attachment to no nation upon earth should supplant our attachment to liberty. This, we flattered ourselves, was the ultimate step of the controversy;
but subsequent events have shewn how vain was this hope of finding mod-
eration in our enemies. . . .

Fruitless were all the entreaties, arguments, and eloquence of an illustrious band of the most distinguished peers and commoners, who nobly
and strenuously asserted the justice of our cause, to stay or even to miti-
gate the heedless fury with which these accumulated and unexampled outrages were hurried on. Equally fruitless was the interference of the City of
London, of Bristol, and many other respectable towns in our favour.
Parliament adopted an insidious manoeuvre calculated to divide us, to
establish a perpetual auction of taxations where colony should bid against
colony, all of them uninformed what ransom would redeem their lives; and
thus to extort from us, at the point of the bayonet, the unknown sums that
should be sufficient to gratify, if possible to gratify ministerial rapacity,
with the miserable indulgence left to us of raising, in our own mode, the
prescribed tribute. What terms more rigid and humiliating could have
been dictated by remorseless victors to conquered enemies? in our circumstances to accept them would be to deserve them. . . .

Our cause is just. Our union is perfect. Our internal resources are great,
and, if necessary, foreign assistance is undoubtedly attainable. We grate-
fully acknowledge, as signal instances of the Divine favour towards us, that
His Providence would not permit us to be called into this severe controversy until we were grown up to our present strength, had been previously exercised in warlike operations, and possessed of the means of defending ourselves. With hearts fortified with these animating reflections, we
most solemnly, before God and the world, *declare*, that exerting the utmost
energy of those powers which our beneficent Creator hath graciously
bestowed upon us, the arms we have been compelled by our enemies to
assume, we will, in defiance of every hazard, with unabating firmness and
perseverance, employ for the preservation of our liberties; being with one
mind resolved to die freemen, rather then to live slaves.

Samuel Eliot Morison, ed., *Sources and Documents Illustrating the American Revolution, 1764–1788, and the
Formation of the Federal Constitution.* Oxford: Clarendon Press, 1953, pp. 141–45.

Document 12: The War Is Justified by Its Glorious Aims

*On July 3, 1776, the day before the historic signing of the Declaration of
Independence, John Adams wrote two letters to his wife, Abigail. In the stirring
lines excerpted here, he reaffirms what he has advocated for some time, that war
with Britain is inevitable and regrettable, but tempers this theme with the more
optimistic note that whatever the new nation must endure will be worth it in the
long run, for in the end Americans will enjoy complete freedom and self-rule.*

Yesterday the greatest question was decided, which ever was debated in America, and a greater perhaps, never was or will be decided among men. . . .

It may be the will of Heaven that America shall suffer calamities still more wasting and distresses yet more dreadful. If this is to be the case, it will have this good effect, at least: it will inspire us with many virtues, which we have not, and correct many errors, follies, and vices, which threaten to disturb, dishonor, and destroy us. The furnace of affliction produces refinement, in states as well as individuals. And the new governments we are assuming, in every part, will require a purification from our vices, and an augmentation of our virtues or they will be no blessings. The people will have unbounded power. And the people are extremely addicted to corruption and venality, as well as the great. I am not without apprehensions from this quarter. But I must submit all my hopes and fears, to an overruling Providence, in which, unfashionable as the faith may be, I firmly believe. . . .

The second day of July 1776, will be the most memorable epocha in the history of America. I am apt to believe that it will be celebrated, by succeeding generations, as the great anniversary festival. It ought to be commemorated as the Day of Deliverance by solemn acts of devotion to God Almighty. It ought to be solemnized with pomp and parade, with shows, games, sports, guns, bells, bonfires, and illuminations from one end of this continent to the other from this time forward forever more.

You will think me transported with Enthusiasm but I am not. I am well aware of the toil and blood and treasure, that it will cost us to maintain this Declaration, and support and defend these States. Yet through all the gloom I can see the rays of ravishing light and glory. I can see that the end is more than worth all the means. And that posterity will triumph in that day's transaction, even although we should rue it, which I trust in God we shall not.

Merrill Jensen, *The Founding of a Nation: A History of the American Revolution, 1763–1776*. New York: Oxford University Press, 1968, pp. 703–704.

Document 13: A Loyalist Claims America Cannot Win the War

On October 8, 1777, loyalist Jacob Duché, rector of Christ Church in Philadelphia, wrote a letter to George Washington, commander of the American army, imploring him to give up the hopeless fight and seek reconciliation with England.

What have been the consequences of this rash & violent measure? A degeneracy of representation—Confusion of Counsels—Blunders without number. The most respectable Characters have withdrawn themselves & are succeeded by a great majority of illiberal & violent men. . . .

O my Dear Sir! What a sad Contrast? Characters now present themselves whose minds can never mingle with your own. Your [Benjamin] Harrison alone remains & he disgusted with his unworthy associates.

As to those of my own province, some of them are so obscure that their very names never met my Ears before, & others have only been distinguished for the weakness of their understandings & the violence of their tempers. . . .

From the New England Provinces can you find one that, as a Gentleman, you could wish to associate with? Unless the soft & mild address of Mr. Hancock can attone for his want of every other qualification necessary for the Station he fills. —Bankrupts, Attornies & men of desperate fortunes are his Colleagues. . . .

Are the dregs of a Congress then still to influence a mind like yours? These are not the men you engaged to serve. These are not the men that America has chosen to represent her. . . .

After this view of Congress turn to the Army. The whole world knows that its very existence depends upon you, that your Death or Captivity disperses it in a moment, & that there is not a man on that side the Question in America capable of succeeding you. As to the Army itself what have you to expect from them? Have they not frequently abandoned even yourself in the hour of extremity? Have you, can you have the least confidence in a set of undisciplined men & Officers, many of whom have been taken from the lowest of the people, without principle, without courage. —Take away those that surround your person, how very few are there that you can ask to sit at your Table? . . .

And now where are your resources? O my Dear Sir! How sadly have you been abused by a faction void of Truth & void of tenderness to you & your Country? They have amused you with hopes of a Declaration of War on the part of France. Believe me from the best authority 'twas a fiction from the first. . . .

From your friends in England you have nothing to expect. . . . The spirit of the whole nation is in full activity against you. . . . All orders & ranks of men in Great Britain are now unanimous & determined to risque their all in the Contest. . . . In a word your Harbours are blocked up, your Cities fall one after another, fortress after fortress, battle after battle is lost. A British army after having passed almost unmolested thro' a vast extent of Country have possessed themselves with ease of the Capital of America. How unique the contest now! How fruitless the expence of Blood! . . .

Your penetrating Eye needs not more explicit Language to discern my meaning. With that prudence & delicacy therefore of which I know you to be possessed represent to Congress the indispensable necessity of rescinding the hasty & ill advised Declaration of Independency. Recommend, & you have an undoubted right to recommend, an immediate cessation of hostilities.

Catherine S. Crary, ed., *The Price of Loyalty: Tory Writings from the Revolutionary Era*. New York: McGraw-Hill, 1973, pp. 156–58.

Document 14: The Seeds of a Social Revolution?

In the 1920s, the distinguished historian J. Franklin Jameson, editor of the American Historical Review *from 1895 to 1928, collected and published four lectures he had delivered at Princeton as* The American Revolution Considered as a Social Movement, *which scholars variously called "a gem of historical writing," "a truly notable book," and a "minor classic." Jameson's thesis, that the political revolution brought about by the American War of Independence set in motion profound social changes that reshaped America, set off a firestorm of scholarly debate and historical reappraisals that has continued, more or less vigorously, to the present. The portions of the book included below begin with Jameson's classic statement of social revolution and then proceed to two of his central examples: how the institution of slavery began to change and how land entail (restrictions forcing property to remain in the hands of the same family generation after generation) and primogeniture (rights of inheritance granted only to the eldest son) were eradicated.*

It is indeed true that our Revolution was strikingly unlike that of France, and that most of those who originated it had no other than a political programme, and would have considered its work done when political independence of Great Britain had been secured. But who can say to the waves of revolution: Thus far shall we go and no farther? The various fibres of a nation's life are knit together in great complexity. It is impossible to sever some without also loosening others, and setting them free to combine anew in widely different forms. The Americans were much more conservative than the French. But their political and their social systems, though both were, as the great orator said, still in the gristle and not yet hardened into the bone of manhood, were too intimately connected to permit that the one should remain unchanged while the other was radically altered. The stream of revolution, once started, could not be confined within narrow banks, but spread abroad upon the land. Many economic desires, many social aspirations were set free by the political struggle, many aspects of colonial society profoundly altered by the forces thus let loose. The relations of social classes to each other, the institution of slavery, the system of land-holding, the course of business, the forms and spirit of the intellectual and religious life, all felt the transforming hand of revolution, all emerged from under it in shapes advanced many degrees nearer to those we know. . . .

Any consideration of the effect of the American Revolution on the status of persons [must address] . . . its influence on the institution of slavery, for at this time the contrast between American freedom and American slavery comes out, for the first time, with startling distinctness. . . .

We may note the organized efforts toward the removal or alleviation of slavery manifested in the creation of a whole group of societies for these purposes. The first anti-slavery society in this or any other country was formed on April 14, 1775, five days before the battle of Lexington, by a meeting at the Sun Tavern, on Second Street in Philadelphia. The members were mostly of the Society of Friends. . . . The New York "Society for Promoting the Manumission of Slaves" was organized in 1785, with John Jay for its first president. In 1788 a society similar to these two was founded in Delaware, and within four years there were other such in Rhode Island, Connecticut, New Jersey, Maryland, and Virginia, and local societies enough to make at least thirteen, mostly in the slave-holding states.

In actual results of the growing sentiment, we may note, first of all, the checking of the importation of slaves, and thus of the horrors of the trans-Atlantic slave trade. The Continental Congress of 1774 had been in session but a few days when they decreed an "American Association," or non-importation agreement, in which one section read: "That we will neither import nor purchase any slave imported after the first day of December next, after which we will wholly discontinue the slave trade, and will neither be concerned in it ourselves, nor will we hire our vessels nor sell our commodities or manufactures to those who are concerned in it"; and the evidence seems to be that the terms of this agreement were enforced throughout the war with little evasion.

States also acted. Four months before this, in July 1774, Rhode Island had passed a law to the effect that all slaves thereafter brought into the colony should be free. . . . A similar law was passed that same year in Connecticut. Delaware prohibited importation in 1776, Virginia in 1778, Maryland in 1783, South Carolina in 1787, for a term of years, and North Carolina, in 1786, imposed a larger duty on each negro imported. . . .

The Superior Court of Massachusetts declared that slavery had been abolished in that state by the mere declaration of its constitution that "all men are born free and equal." In 1784 Connecticut and Rhode Island passed acts which gradually extinguished slavery. In other states, ameliorations of the law respecting slaves were effected even though the abolition of slavery could not be brought about. Thus in 1782 Virginia passed an act which provided that any owner might, by an instrument properly attested, freely manumit all his slaves, if he gave security that their maintenance should not become a public charge. It may seem but a slight thing, this law making private manumission easy where before it had been difficult. But it appears to have led in eight years to the freeing of more than ten thousand slaves, twice as great a number as were freed by reason of the Massachusetts constitution, and as many as there were in Rhode Island and Connecticut together when the war broke out. . . .

Thus in many ways the successful struggle for the independence of the United States affected the character of American society by altering the status of persons. . . .

If, as I have suggested, nothing was more important in the American social system than its relation to the land, and if the Revolution had any social effects at all, we should expect to see it overthrowing any old-fashioned features which still continued to exist in the land laws. What, then, was the old land-law in the American colonies? The feudal ages had discovered that, if men desired to give stability to society by keeping property in the hands of the same families generation after generation, the best way to do this was to entail the lands strictly, so that the holder could not sell them or even give them away, and to have a law of primogeniture, which, in case the father made no will, would turn over all his lands to the eldest son, to the exclusion of all the other children. There could not be two better devices for forming and maintaining a landholding aristocracy. . . .

In ten years from the Declaration of Independence every state had abolished entails excepting two, and those were two in which entails were rare. In fifteen years every state, without exception, abolished primogeniture and in some form provided for equality of inheritance, since which time the American eldest son has never been a privileged character. . . .

Now I submit that this was not an accident. How hard Washington found it to get these thirteen legislatures to act together! And yet here we find them all with one accord making precisely the same changes in their land-laws. Such uniformity must have had a common cause, and where shall we find it if we do not admit that our Revolution, however much it differed from the French Revolution in spirit, yet carried in itself the seeds of a social revolution?

J. Franklin Jameson, *The American Revolution Considered as a Social Movement*. Princeton, NJ: Princeton University Press, 1926, pp. 9–38, passim.

CHRONOLOGY

1756–1763
Britain and France fight the Seven Years' War, known in America as the French and Indian War; Britain is victorious and the Treaty of Paris is signed on February 10, 1763; burdened by war debt, the British government begins to see the American colonies as a potential source of new revenue.

1764
On April 5, Parliament passes the Revenue Act (or Sugar Act), placing taxes on sugar, wine, silk, and other luxury items imported into the colonies; most colonies issue mild protests; in August, Boston merchants pledge to boycott British luxury goods and some towns in other colonies follow suit.

1765
On March 22, Parliament passes the Stamp Act, providing for a direct, internal tax on the American colonies; on May 29, the Virginia legislature, inspired in large degree by the oratory of Patrick Henry, passes resolutions condemning the Stamp Act; in October, the Stamp Act Congress, made up of delegates from nine colonies, meets in New York City and petitions Parliament to repeal the Stamp Act; meanwhile, groups of irate citizens in many cities use violence and intimidation to combat implementation of the tax.

1766
Parliament repeals the Stamp Act on March 18.

1767
On June 29, Britain enacts the Townshend Acts, which levy duties on a number of goods entering the colonies; many colonists protest and some organize boycotts of British goods; in November, John Dickinson of Philadelphia begins publishing his "Farmer's Letters," claiming that the Townshend duties are intended to raise revenue and that they interfere with local representative government.

1770
On March 5, five colonists die in Boston when fired on by a squad of British troops; the so-called Boston Massacre becomes a rallying point for the growing ranks of anti-British American patriots; Britain removes the Townshend duties on April 12, except for the tax on imported tea.

1773

On May 10, Parliament passes the Tea Act, which allows the East India Company to bypass British duties and sell its tea more cheaply in America; Philadelphia, New York, and Charleston deny the tea ships permission to dock; in Boston, the ships are allowed to dock but not to unload the tea; on December 16, disgruntled colonists dressed as Indians board the tea ships in Boston harbor and dump the tea into the water, an incident that becomes known as the Boston Tea Party.

1774

Outraged by the destruction of the tea, between March and June Parliament passes the Coercive Acts (known in the colonies as the Intolerable Acts), closing Boston's port and placing severe limitations on local government; on May 17, George Washington, Thomas Jefferson, Patrick Henry, and other Virginia patriots meet in Williamsburg and declare that an attack on one colony will be interpreted as an attack on all; in September, the First Continental Congress meets in Philadelphia to decide what to do about the Coercive Acts; meanwhile, on September 9, a meeting of several towns in the Boston area passes the Suffolk Resolves, which condemn the Coercive Acts and call for Massachusetts to form its own government in defiance of the royal governor and also for people to begin arming themselves in preparation for possible fighting; on learning of the Suffolk Resolves, the congress endorses them and on October 14 passes its own resolves, condemning the Coercive Acts and agreeing to meet again the following year if Britain continues to abuse colonial rights.

1775

On January 20, British parliamentary leader William Pitt warns his colleagues that if Britain does not back off, the Americans will fight and that the mother country will ultimately lose its American colonies; Pitt's warning goes unheeded, tensions continue to rise, and on April 19, a British force fires on colonial militiamen in Lexington and Concord, villages outside of Boston, initiating open hostilities between Britain and America; on May 10, the Second Continental Congress convenes in Philadelphia; in June, British and American soldiers clash in the Battle of Bunker Hill (actually fought on Breed's Hill) in Boston, where the British suffer heavy casualties.

1776

In January, American patriot Thomas Paine calls for the colonies to seek independence from Britain in his pamphlet *Common Sense*, which sells over one hundred thousand copies in only three months and strongly influences colonial opinion; meanwhile, ongoing persecution of American loyalists, who believe that the colonists should remain British subjects, increases and many loyalists flee the colonies; on July 4, the members of Congress sign the Declaration of Independence, recently drafted by Thomas Jefferson, marking the official birth of a new nation—the United States of America.

1776–1779
The war rages mainly in the middle colonies; the British occupy Yorktown, in Virginia, and Philadelphia.

1777
Congress drafts the Articles of Confederation, constituting a temporary plan for a federal government; Congress also recommends that the states raise revenue by selling loyalist property; America's Horatio Gates delivers Britain's General Burgoyne a humiliating defeat at Saratoga, New York, marking the conflict's turning point in America's favor.

1778
On February 6, encouraged by the American victory at Saratoga, France concludes a military alliance with the United States.

1779
By signing a treaty with France, Spain offers its indirect support for the American Revolution.

1779–1781
The main theater of the war shifts to the southern states.

1781
On October 19, finding himself surrounded at Yorktown by combined American-French forces under General George Washington, Britain's General Charles Cornwallis surrenders his 7,247 troops, marking the end of the last major battle of the Revolutionary War.

1782
The preliminary peace treaty is concluded on November 30.

1783
On September 3, representatives of the warring parties sign the final version of the peace treaty.

STUDY QUESTIONS

Chapter 1

1. Explain what writers like Soame Jenyns and Thomas Whately (Viewpoint 1) mean by "virtual" representation. Would you be willing to settle for this sort of representation in today's U.S. Congress? Why or why not?

2. According to Daniel Dulany and William Pitt (Viewpoint 2), how is raising money through an "internal" tax different than doing so through trade regulations?

3. What are Daniel Dulany's arguments (Viewpoint 2) refuting virtual representation?

4. Compare Stephen Hopkins's views (Viewpoint 3) about rights granted in the original colonial charters with those of Francis Bernard (Viewpoint 4).

5. Cite some of Henry Caner's complaints (Viewpoint 4) about the Sons of Liberty. In your opinion, are his views reasonable given the circumstances of his time? Why or why not?

Chapter 2

1. List at least five reasons given in Viewpoint 1 justifying a break between Britain and the American colonies.

2. What are the immediate advantages of independence, as cited by John Adams in Viewpoint 1? What long-term advantages does Jacob Green cite? How did some of Green's prophecies eventually come true?

3. According to Viewpoint 2, why did many American loyalists choose to flee the colonies? In your opinion, was their treatment at the hands of patriots justified or unjustified? Why?

4. According to Charles Inglis (Viewpoint 2), what are the advantages of reconciling with the mother country?

Chapter 3

1. According to the Reverend Samuel Seabury (Viewpoint 1), what is the right course for the American colonies to take?

2. Both patriots and loyalists invoked the name of God, each side suggesting that the Creator supported its views and aims. Compare the statements to this effect by the Quakers (Viewpoint 1) and Thomas Paine (Viewpoint 4).

3. What advice does Jacob Duché give George Washington in Viewpoint 1? Based on what you know about American history, did Washington follow this advice?

4. List at least four reasons given in Viewpoint 2 that a war with Britain is justified.

5. What reasons do Charles Inglis and Jacob Duché give (Viewpoint 3) for America's certain defeat in a war with Britain?

6. In Viewpoint 4, what major British disadvantage does Edmund Burke cite?

7. According to Mr. Adair (Viewpoint 4), what would be the result of a British victory in the war?

Chapter 4

1. What, according to Viewpoint 1, made American revolutionaries radical for their time?

2. Name some groups cited in Viewpoint 1 that eventually demanded and gained their rights in American society. Research the struggle of one of these groups and write a three-to-four-page report summarizing that struggle.

3. Why, according to Clinton Rossiter in Viewpoint 2, were the leaders of the American Revolution conservative rather than radical revolutionaries?

4. Discuss how the main arguments of Viewpoints 1 and 2 might be reconciled by this supposition: "The American War of Independence was not a social revolution at the time, but its core ideals inevitably led to one." Cite examples from the two essays, as well as from other sources.

For Further Reading

Isaac Asimov, *The Birth of the United States, 1763–1816.* Boston: Houghton Mifflin, 1974. One of the most prolific and gifted of American popular writers here delivers a highly informative survey of the main events and characters of the American Revolution and early decades of the United States.

Bruce Bliven Jr., *The American Revolution.* New York: Random House, 1986. A commendable synopsis of the U.S. War of Independence, aimed at middle school readers.

Nardi R. Campion, *Patrick Henry: Firebrand of the Revolution.* Boston: Little, Brown, 1961. A general biography of the Virginia legislator whose patriotic oratory helped to inspire much revolutionary fervor in the American colonies. For middle school readers.

Margaret Cousins, *Ben Franklin of Old Philadelphia.* New York: Random House, 1980. The main events and characters of the tumultuous years leading up to the Declaration of Independence are captured in this biography of one of the principal Founding Fathers. Aimed at middle school readers.

Bonnie L. Lukes, *The American Revolution.* San Diego: Lucent Books, 1996. A well-written history of the American War of Independence, highlighted by numerous quotes from primary and secondary historical and literary sources describing the conflict and the period. Suitable for middle school, high school, and adult nonspecialist readers.

Don Nardo, *Thomas Jefferson.* San Diego: Lucent Books, 1993; *Democracy* and *The U.S. Congress,* both San Diego: Lucent Books, 1994; and *The U.S. Presidency.* San Diego: Lucent Books, 1995. These books, geared for the middle and high school reading level but accessible to all general readers, provide useful overviews of the essentials of the American government, its creation, structure, strengths, limitations, and most memorable leaders.

Don Nardo, *The Bill of Rights.* San Diego: Greenhaven Press, 1997. This informative book serves as a useful companion volume to *The American Revolution,* providing a comparable collection of extensively documented essays containing a wide range of opinions and debates about American rights.

131

Walter Olesky, *The Boston Tea Party*. New York: Franklin Watts, 1993. The events and personalities shaping the famous incident that provoked Parliament into punishing Boston and thereby fatally escalated tensions between the colonies and Britain are recounted here in a simple format for basic readers.

Gail B. Stewart, *The Revolutionary War*. San Diego: Lucent Books, 1991. One of the best current writers for young adults does a fine job chronicling the main events of the war between Britain and its American colonies. Constitutes another useful companion volume to *The American Revolution*.

Irwin Unger, *These United States: The Questions of Our Past*. Vol. 1. Boston: Little, Brown, 1978. Aimed at high school and undergraduate college students, this is one of the best available general, nonscholarly histories of the early United States. Very well written, with excellent production values.

Brian Williams, *George Washington*. New York: Marshall Cavendish, 1988. The events leading to the founding of the United States and beyond are traced in this general biography of the Revolutionary War general and first U.S. president. Reading level is middle school.

MAJOR WORKS CONSULTED

Primary Sources

The following volumes (or sets of volumes) are large, comprehensive, and invaluable mines of primary source materials, each containing from several dozen to more than a hundred complete or partial documents (letters, pamphlets, newspaper articles, journals, town records, and so on) from the formative era of the United States.

Bernard Bailyn, ed., *Pamphlets of the American Revolution.* Cambridge, MA: Harvard University Press, 1965.

Max Beloff, ed., *The Debate on the American Revolution, 1761–1783.* London: Adam and Charles Black, 1960.

Henry S. Commager and Richard B. Morris, eds., *The Spirit of 'Seventy-Six: The Story of the American Revolution as Told by Participants.* 2 vols. New York: Bobbs-Merrill, 1958.

Catherine S. Crary, ed., *The Price of Loyalty: Tory Writings from the Revolutionary Era.* New York: McGraw-Hill, 1973.

John C. Dann, ed., *The Revolution Remembered: Eyewitness Accounts of the War for Independence.* Chicago: University of Chicago Press, 1980.

William Dudley, ed., *The American Revolution.* San Diego: Greenhaven Press, 1992.

Samuel Eliot Morison, ed., *Sources and Documents Illustrating the American Revolution, 1764–1788, and the Formation of the Federal Constitution.* Oxford: Clarendon Press, 1953.

Richard B. Morris, ed., *The American Revolution, 1763–1783: A Bicentennial Collection.* Columbia: University of South Carolina Press, 1970.

Howard H. Peckham, ed., *Sources of American Independence.* 2 vols. Chicago: University of Chicago Press, 1978.

Leslie F.S. Upton, ed., *Revolutionary Versus Loyalist.* Waltham, MA: Blaisdell, 1968.

Alden T. Vaughan, ed., *Chronicles of the Revolution.* New York: Grosset and Dunlap, 1965.

Major Modern Sources

David Ammerman, *In Common Cause: American Response to the Coercive Acts of 1774*. Charlottesville: University Press of Virginia, 1974. An excellent scholarly study of the institution of and reactions to the British measures, called the Intolerable Acts by the colonists, that placed severe restrictions on Boston as retaliation for the Boston Tea Party.

Robert M. Calhoon, *The Loyalists in Revolutionary America, 1760–1781*. New York: Harcourt Brace Jovanovich, 1973. The most comprehensive and informative single-volume study available of the American loyalists and their often tragic plight, as they found themselves caught between allegiance to the mother country and the rise of revolutionary fervor around them.

Edward Countryman, *The American Revolution*. New York: Hill and Wang, 1985. Arguably the most authoritative single-volume general history of the American War of Independence, this is a large, richly documented, and engrossing study. Highly recommended.

Eric Foner, *Tom Paine and Revolutionary America*. New York: Oxford University Press, 1976. This biography of the fiery revolutionary who penned the widely influential *Common Sense* effectively covers the social and political panorama of the American colonies of his era. Well written, superbly documented, and generally superior among its kind.

Merrill Jensen, *The Founding of a Nation: A History of the American Revolution, 1763–1776*. New York: Oxford University Press, 1968. Jensen, one of the major historians of the revolutionary period, here explores the writings, speeches, actions, and reactions of the colonists in the formative years of the founding of the United States.

Edmund S. Morgan and Helen M. Morgan, *The Stamp Act Crisis: Prologue to Revolution*. Chapel Hill: University of North Carolina Press, 1953. A highly detailed and comprehensive scholarly study of the background of the Stamp Act, British motivations for implementing it, America's irate reactions to enactment, the act's repeal, and how the crisis foreshadowed the coming struggle between the colonies and the mother country.

Hugh F. Rankin, *The American Revolution*. New York: G.P. Putnam's Sons, 1964. Rankin, formerly of Tulane University, here effectively covers the highlights of the U.S. War of Independence through a chain of long, colorful, and often dramatic eyewitness accounts (each preceded by an informative preface by the author).

Clinton Rossiter, *Seedtime of the Republic: The Origin of the American Tradition of Political Liberty*. New York: Harcourt, Brace and World, 1953. The widely respected former Cornell University scholar won a number of literary awards for this study, an original in its time, which examines the political ideas that shaped the American Revolution and how those ideas became part of the fabric of the documents and institutions of the infant United States.

Harry M. Ward, *The American Revolution: Nationhood Achieved, 1763–1788*. New York: St. Martin's Press, 1995. A fine, up-to-date, quite detailed overview of the American march toward independence, the struggle with Britain, and the early formative years of the new American nation.

Additional Works Consulted

George A. Billias, ed., *The American Revolution: How Revolutionary Was It?* New York: Holt, Rinehart, and Winston, 1965.

Colin Bonwick, *English Radicals and the American Revolution*. Chapel Hill: University of North Carolina Press, 1977.

Philip Davidson, *Propaganda and the American Revolution, 1763–1783*. New York: W.W. Norton, 1973.

Joseph J. Ellis, *American Sphinx: The Character of Thomas Jefferson*. New York: Knopf, 1997.

Thomas Flemming, *1776: Year of Illusion*. New York: Norton, 1975.

Thomas Flexner, *George Washington*. Boston: Little, Brown, 1968.

Robert Gross, *The Minutemen and Their World*. New York: Hill and Wang, 1976.

Richard Hofstadter et al., *The United States: The History of a Republic*. Englewood Cliffs, NJ: Prentice-Hall, 1957.

J. Franklin Jameson, *The American Revolution Considered as a Social Movement*. Princeton, NJ: Princeton University Press, 1926.

Piers Mackesy, *The War for America, 1775–1783*. Cambridge, MA: Harvard University Press, 1964.

Pauline Maier, *From Resistance to Revolution*. New York: Knopf, 1972.

Samuel Eliot Morison, *The Oxford History of the American People*. New York: Oxford University Press, 1965.

Diane Ravitch, ed., *The American Reader: Words That Moved a Nation*. New York: HarperCollins, 1990.

John Shy, *Toward Lexington: The Role of the British Army in the Coming of the American Revolution*. Princeton, NJ: Princeton University Press, 1965.

John Shy, *A People Numerous and Armed: Reflections on the Military Struggle for American Independence*. New York: Oxford University Press, 1976.

Robert W. Tucker and David C. Hendrickson, *The Fall of the First British Empire*. Baltimore: Johns Hopkins University Press, 1982.

John C. Wahlke, ed., *The Causes of the American Revolution*. Boston: D.C. Heath, 1950.

Francis G. Walett, *Patriots, Loyalists, and Printers: Bicentennial Articles on the American Revolution.* Worcester, MA: American Antiquarian Society, 1976.

Gordon S. Wood, *The Radicalism of the American Revolution.* New York: Knopf, 1992.

Howard Zinn, *A People's History of the United States.* New York: HarperCollins, 1980.

INDEX

ABOUT THE AUTHOR

Historian and award-winning author Don Nardo has written many books for young adults about American history and government, including *The U.S. Presidency, The U.S. Congress, The Mexican-American War, The Bill of Rights, The Great Depression,* and *Franklin D. Roosevelt: U.S. President.* Mr. Nardo has also written several teleplays and screenplays, including work for Warner Brothers and ABC-Television. He lives with his wife, Christine, and dog, Bud, on Cape Cod, Massachusetts.